A QUEST FOR ST. JAMES

A Country Boy's Transformation

TOMMY RAY

GRATITUDE

I wish to express gratitude and thankfulness for this pilgrimage.

For my first night in St. Jean de Porte, France, a safe place was given to sleep when all other accommodations were full, as the clock struck midnight.

To my fellow pilgrims who offered support, love, and a Buen Camino!

To my friend from Germany, Michael, with whom I walked almost the entire route, from St. Jean to Santiago and onward to Finisterre and Muxia.

To the Canadian woman whose generosity brought tears to my eyes in a restaurant with her gift, which allowed me to eat along my Camino.

To my friends from North Carolina, Joe, and Celina, whom were always there to give me a hug, a kind word, and supporting words. Observing their love for each other instilled what I hope to have in my marriage someday.

I thank God who kept me protected, provided for my needs, and helped me complete my journey of over 600 miles.

DISCLAIMER

In October 2012, I completed the Camino de Santiago, the way of St. James, the ancient pilgrim path of the Camino Frances, with a continuation to Finisterre and Muxia. *A Quest for St. James* chronicled the pilgrimage.

A Quest for St. James reflect my opinions and experiences. The overall adventure transpired overwhelming. However, from the times of aches and soreness to bliss and joy, from tears to euphoria, the overall comradery along the Camino and the friends you meet make all of the trials worth it.

I have changed some names along with identifying details of individuals mentioned in the book to protect their privacy.

"Adventure should be part of everyone's life. It is the whole difference between being fully alive and just existing."
—Holly Morris

CHAPTER 1

As the alarm sounded, I craved to sleep longer. Perhaps, with more time on the pillow, clarity would surface. Last night, with only an ivory sheet shrouding my body, beads of perspiration enveloped me forcing constant tossing, and turning, clutching the sheet while I pondered, reflected, and speculated. I marveled at what trekking the Camino de Santiago would actually be like. Am I capable to do it? Or foolish thinking of such a concept? All night long the mind raced from one image to another. The internal battle of "Go for it!" versus "You're crazy!" clashed. It battled until the blackness relinquished into various shades of gray, until dawn.

I recall when I arrived at work that day. I quietly and sluggishly changed into my scrubs with brief good mornings to the surgical team. The decision weighing heavily on me. Throughout the morning cases on Wednesday, I remained low key. I dropped an instrument during one case as my mind drifted away for a second.

After a few back-to-back surgical procedures, I located Dr. Palm Harbor sitting in the lounge area. I walked over, about to ask to speak with him privately when. . .

CHAPTER 2

O ver the past six months, something changed inside of my mind, like a mysterious energy guiding my direction of thought. I was in a healthy place, have worked in orthopedic surgery as a physician assistant for over three years, and part of the medical staff of two major league baseball teams. My boss and I were close friends with a professional relationship built on trust and respect. I owned a house, a brand-new truck, and just started dating someone. I lived within ten minutes of my three older brothers, my mom as well as many friends. Negatives existed of course; the office politics, the continuous fifty-five-hour-plus work weeks, and the deepness of debt because of school loans of over $200,000. On the surface, most said my current life was a dream, a goal for many to strive to achieve. However, my mind and heart spoke a different language. I believed I was unsatisfied with the locked in routine, no longer desiring to be a hamster on a wheel.

I understood you only had one shot at life, believing in a special magic in our existence which should be tapped into. I trusted life should not be taken for granted, instead to become the best version of yourself. I knew I should listen to my heart above all else. I yearned for a quest to fulfill my destiny trusting nothing was impossible. I must rely on my own instincts. Yes, I have a purpose.

"If you don't know where you are going, you might wind up someplace else." —Yogi Berra

CHAPTER 3

ORIGINS

B orn in Zama, Mississippi, in the year of 1973. A small town between Kosciusko and Philadelphia, down a red dusty dirt country road. The population had around 36 people.

My father was a pipeliner. A pipeliner was anyone working on a job site installing either gas lines or water lines. He operated a large track hoe or backhoe depending on the size of the task. He had to travel a lot for his occupation. In the beginning, my mom and I followed him around the country from job to job, living in motels or rental mobile homes. Based on the lifestyle, I attended three different kindergartens, two different first grades, and two different second grade classes. The ability to adapt to change imprinted early on my child's mind. Finally, we attempted to settle in Zama, where I began the third grade. My father remained away most of the time.

As your imagination can picture, our town was teensy. The two towns mentioned above were almost 35–45

minutes away in opposite directions. In Zama, we had a store carrying basic needs of food and supplies. It had two gas pumps, which made
it a popular stopping point for the country folk in the area. We lived with my Granny Ray in a home built at the turn of the century. My aunt, uncle, and one cousin lived across the street. I can remember when my Granny had indoor plumbing installed when I was four or five. Up to that point, we used an outhouse. Located up another dirt road, our school, a church, an abandoned sawmill, and cemetery. At the school I attended, the same teacher taught the third and fourth grade at the same time. We had eight fourth graders and six third graders in the same classroom.

However, after a few months, my mom missed her home in North Carolina. So, she packed me up, and we moved. I remained in North Carolina from the third grade through undergrad at Guilford College. The time spent there was the longest I resided in one state. During the stay, I lived in over ten different apartments or mobile homes. A continual reminder of the lack of stability.

Instead of using the history of instability as a crutch, I thrived from growing up in multiple states. I discovered many things, the good along with the bad, and interacted with diverse people from a young age. It allowed me to have an open mind about all walks of life. The unorthodox foundation imprinted a path for me to always desire adventure and to pursue my dreams and goals. I recognized the difference of what life could be like without an education.

After 15 years of my first profession, as a certified athletic trainer. I decided I could accomplish far more in life.

Through many blessings and support from friends, I reduced to part-time work to perform the required pre-requisites for a physician assistant program. Over a span of 15 months, I attended classes to qualify. Graduating from the program 27-months later, comprised the culmination of my third degree and second master's degree. An excellent physician named Dr. Palm Harbor, based in Florida hired me two weeks before graduating. He was one of the best technical surgeons I have ever seen. He could perform his surgeries quicker than or with better technical precision than most surgeons from around the world. The incredible opportunity had an added blessing, I provided medical care for two professional baseball teams.

Unfortunately, as time passed, the amount of stress began taking its toll on my physical and mental states. After three years, I sensed a need for some time off, an extended vacation. I normally would take a few days here and there or add an extra day to a holiday season. However, I never traveled somewhere amazing. I swiftly learned in the medical field the longer absent from the office, the worse it was when returning. Not only did you have to catch up from not seeing patients but the towers of paperwork in the in-box. It was easier to remain and appreciate a light day or your weekend instead of traveling. Tragically, it leads to becoming like a mouse chasing cheese in a maze.

I declared: I am a self-reliant spirit. I shall continue to do what was best for me along my journey understanding what was best may actually not be the easiest option. I trusted I walked on the correct path.

Finally, I committed to a 10-day vacation.

I began researching 10-day excursions. I looked for something to cross off my bucket list like shark diving or a journey around Costa Rica. Unfortunately, they turned out to be too expensive. Then one night, I watched a movie which provided me my answer: *The Way*, directed by Emilio Estevez. It starred his father, Martin Sheen. They created the premise of the movie around the Camino de Santiago.

I instantly connected with Emilio Estevez's character. An educated man not following the norm society has attempted to force upon us. He understood a marvelous world awaited him out there. It meant life was to gain experiences, more importantly, to live. Though not considered an inspirational film. The movie procured acclamations as a spiritual feat, as it followed the steps of St. James.

I believed it struck an inner chord of my heart because of my similar desire to travel. It provided an experience to regain the important aspect I was longing for. I desired to rediscover my inner voice, my instincts, which faded with the daily grind. I sensed a true internal personal transformation could occur after completing the Camino de Santiago. I trusted it would be a journey of discovery and fulfilment for me. The movie's picturesque adventure ignited a passion. I desired my blue eyes to gaze upon those same landscapes.

The Camino de Santiago, or *The Way of St. James*, is a network of pilgrimage trails to the ultimate destination of Santiago in Spain. In Santiago, they say they buried the remains of the Apostle Saint James in the Cathedral of Santiago de Compostela. Saint James designated the patron saint of Spain. James, one of only three apostles whom Jesus selected to bear witness to his transfiguration. According to legend, his body, along with his followers, sailed to the Iberian Peninsula on a rudderless ship with no sail. Landing on the northwest coast of the peninsula, they proceeded up the River Ulla to land at Iria Flavia (modern-day Padron). The Celtic Queen Lupia ruled those lands, and when asked by James's followers if they could bury his body, she refused and sent troops after them. While chasing the followers of James with his body across a bridge, it collapsed, killing her troops. Queen Lupia then converted to Christianity and provided an ox and cart to transport the body. Unsure of where they should bury the sacred remains, his followers prayed on this and decided to let the ox continue until it chooses a place to rest. After pausing at a stream, the ox finally came to rest under an oak tree at the top of a hill. The ox's location is where the Cathedral of Santiago stands today.

Most walkers/hikers/trekkers/pilgrims use the experience of the Camino for spiritual growth. The length of the pilgrimage depended on the choice of route. Most routes are of at least 500 miles. A Google search offered over one hundred million sites to choose from to learn the history or any other facet you wanted to know about the paths.

The original plan forged was to travel for a 10-day pilgrimage. An added benefit of walking the Camino de Santiago, the Compostela. The Compostela, a certificate of accomplishment once you have completed at least 100 km

(62 miles) by foot. I thought the distance would be doable in 10 days.

Over the next few weeks, I continued researching articles along with joining forums online to speak with people from around the world who either already completed it or were in their own planning stages. Gathering towers of information, I decided 10 days would not be enough to accomplish my vision. An internal flame raged. With considerable prayer and a sense of urgency to experience life, I decided to walk the entire route. I believed I should experience the full Camino de Santiago. However, the decision to complete the total route meant I would have to resign my position with Dr. Palm Harbor so I would have no time limit for its completion.

Once I chose to experience the whole Camino, I booked a one-way flight to Spain. The departure date set for September, four months away. The next step inform my boss of my decision.

CHAPTER 4

CLEAR MIND

*At that exact moment, the next surgical procedure
broadcasted over the loudspeaker. He smiled at me: "How
about we walk and talk?"*

D r. Palm Harbor and I have worked together now for
three years. I was his physician assistant. Up to that
point, I have lasted longer as his PA-C than any other PA
he has had in his 20-year career. I handled his type A personality, the rigors of the long hours, as well as assist him
to ease his daily work life. We as well formed a bond of
friendship. He invited me on fishing trips, I became part
of his social network meeting his friends and invitations to
celebrations. I called him my friend. He understood I had
introverted ways, always searching for "something." He
sensed my desire to not live in a box.

Standing side by side at our scrub sink, I mentioned my
plan. He paused sterilizing his hands. Taken back with my
technique of resignation. In hindsight, it was probably not

the most ideal situation to give him the news. However, I am known to be impulsive when something weighs heavily on my heart. I had to let it out and let him know my thoughts. Dr. Palm Harbor was such a thoughtful mentor that he went home that evening and viewed *The Way*. After watching the movie, he appreciated what inspired me about the pilgrimage. He understood where I was in my life. He agreed, the Camino de Santiago was the best step for me.

We spoke about options for a return to work afterwards. Nonetheless, I decided after the pilgrimage to move on to other endeavors upon further conversations. I presumed upon my return; I would desire new scenery. While a little unnerving to know there was no job (or paycheck) awaiting my return, the freedom meant my trip had no time limit or agenda. I could remain present. I frankly relied on faith all would be well.

From that moment on, I commenced to make the pilgrimage a reality. I began researching the possible financial expenses required for a trip of that magnitude. I purchased a highly recommended guidebook, *A Pilgrim's Guide to The Camino de Santiago* by John Brierley, and I started purchasing supplies. I continued to read the online forums to gain more knowledge. With the gathered wisdom, I mapped out the entire pilgrimage. I knew where to stay, places to visit, as well as things I desired to try. I knew, not only the Camino a geographical journey, but a personal one.

The ultimate step, saying goodbye to someone special. I decided to leave for my pilgrimage four months before the departure date. I had to provide a 90-day resignation notification at work. After I decided on the pilgrimage, I met a wonderful woman and we began dating. What started off as casual, rapidly intensified to a relationship. As time approached for departure, it became difficult to leave her. I must admit, if I had known her before viewing *The Way*, I might still be going to work tomorrow. I hoped on my return she would still be there with open arms. But the unknown was ahead. With a one-way flight to France and over 500 miles of trekking, I had no idea when I would return.

Some readers may ask why I did not change my mind, keep the job, and ensure the relationship continued. Weirdly enough, the thought never crossed my mind. Perhaps I had blind faith she would be picking me up at the airport afterwards. I set in motion an adventure. Nothing was detouring my plan. I committed to the Camino. The pull of rediscovering myself was stronger than following the norm.

Lying supine with her head on my chest, I thought how I made the trip a reality. I resigned my position, planned a pilgrimage, all within a four-month span. I trusted God knew when to put thoughts upon our hearts and to reinforce listening to our instincts. It was my requirement to maintain unwavering faith and purely believe. I fell asleep my final night holding her.

CHAPTER 5

IT'S A NEW DAY

The passenger door opened as I exited the car. She pressed the trunk closed, then twirled around to me. A tear upon her cheek caught my attention. After an embrace of love, I departed into the terminal. I contemplated the four months of preparations and planning. A brief time to change an entire life. I smirked toward the many who commented on my foolishness. Yet, I believed you must follow your heart no matter the situation. Life was fleeting. You must live out your dreams.

Sitting in the dark blue cushioned seat at my terminal, I waited for the boarding call. I prayed the trip would do something amazing for me. I truly sensed God wanted me to walk the Camino. However, sitting there alone in the airport, nervousness shrouded me like a blanket. *Do not be scared,* I told myself. *Have hope and faith. Everything happens for a purpose. Trust the likeliness of having your dreams come true. That makes life interesting.*

My volatile mind wandered back to the plans before me. I had no idea how to speak French. I prayed it would not be a problem when I arrived in Paris. I assumed it would be effortless to locate a hotel upon arrival near the train station for the next day's departure to St. Jean de Port. I expected it would be simple to visit the city after I checked in, considering the accessibility because of their wonderful public transportation system.

Then I thought ahead to the train ride from Paris to St. Jean Pied de Port. I had never ridden on a public train. It would be, yet another, completely novel experience. I booked online, but was my ticket good? How do you check-in for a train? Like a flight? Would I become train sick?

Then thoughts rolled to the Camino itself. I have never trekked before, especially not over 500 miles. Was my backpack too heavy? I attempted to keep the weight down on my pack, as the online forums suggested, to around 14 pounds. Dejectedly, I ended up with a pack weighing between 25 and 30 pounds.

Finally, in those last moments before boarding, to calm my trembling hands, I began people watching—wondering where each person may be going, what they were thinking, or whether they were on their own personal pilgrimage to some exotic destination in our world. And although I was still in my country, the international terminal of the Miami airport bustled with people, fashion, and languages from all over the world.

I decided I would remain in the present moment, take one day at a time, by savoring each day, and attempt unknown things. To drink in each new day and pray it inspired as well as quenched my thirst. I had such grand hopes for my-self. Not only for that trip, but for my life upon my return.

I noticed the space around me becoming crowded. The time to board approached.

I still cannot believe I did it. But I know in reality, many people cannot do such a thing as this. I am truly blessed and grateful. I prayed I see the world differently during and after the adventure. I concluded I wanted my spirit to be freer, not conforming to our society. May every step be a prayer for peace and an extension of loving kindness.

Tampa, Florida to Paris, France

CHAPTER 6

SEPTEMBER 6, 2012

The morning sun was upon us as we touched down in the City of Lights—the first time I ever set foot on foreign soil. After taxiing for a few minutes on the runway, the plane stopped at our arrival gate. The seatbelt sign remained on. After sitting for a few anxious minutes, the police boarded our plane and began walking the aisles. Within seconds, other officers joined the gathering. They seemed to be searching for something or someone on our plane. Or was that the normal protocol for arriving flights? Without a statement, they departed our plane. The seatbelt light disappeared with its chime. We were free to stand, to gather our belongings, and exit the flight. I reached into the overhead compartment to grab my backpack. I only had my backpack on that adventure. It was to act as my everything for the journey.

I desired to open my eyes to all the possibilities along with God's Spirit.

I strolled through the airport, my legs thankful to be upright after an eight-and-a-half-hour flight. The next step, secure a hotel for the night. I attempted to use the information board in the airport about nearby accommodations and even asked a fellow passenger who fortunately spoke English. Regrettably, he could not help me locate a hotel. Slightly downcast, I pressed on. I spotted a help desk. I told the gentleman sitting at the desk my story. Using my cost parameters and desire to be near the train station, he discovered a lovely hotel named Campaihile. A bonus of the hotel, it offered a free brief shuttle trip from the airport. With a sense of relief, the journey continued. I was secure, for at least one night.

I changed clothes and ventured toward the city. Happily, the person at the front desk spoke English. He informed me how to properly locate the subway station and navigate into the heart of Paris without becoming lost. By being a country boy from Zama, Mississippi, I never in my lifetime stepped onto a subway system. I was adventurous, and I was on my pilgrimage. So, this country boy jumped on the subway and started heading for the Eiffel Tower.

The unfortunate aspect about the subway system, at least on that day, the train offered no air-conditioning. It was uncomfortable on the train with temperatures outside in the 90s. Sweat beads formed on my neck along with an uneasiness of my stomach. If I had known about the heat, perhaps, I would have waited until the sun had sunk lower in the sky before my departure.

After a half-hour train ride, I exited the subway station. I climbed up the stairs into a blue-sky day. Standing on a concrete sidewalk of Paris, France, I recognized right away the vast amount of people from all over the world. The air saturated with foreign languages.

The location I entered the city placed me along a canal a few blocks away from the Eiffel Tower. There were a few house boats docked along the path below the sidewalk over a wall. In the distance, a bridge filled with traffic crossing back and forth.

As I began the walk towards the Tower, a local festival unfolded. Live music filled the air as people sold trinkets from small carts or booths, along with souvenirs on the sidewalk. Without looking too much like a tourist, I headed toward the landmarks I desired to see. It amazed me at the lengthy lines to climb the stairs. I had the desire to climb it myself, but not the patience to wait in the heat to attempt it. Instead, I observed from various angles from the ground. I reveled in the scenery for approximately 30 minutes, cherishing the aromas and the surrounding beauty. Then headed back toward the subway station for my next stop: Notre Dame.

Exiting at the second destination, I briefly walked around an open park which contained statues and street performers. As I strolled, I turned my thoughts to food. I wanted to drink and consume local delicacies.

Overtaken by hunger, I could feel the curtain of the headache approaching, as I advanced to the entrance of the restaurant. I no longer viewed Paris for enjoyment. Instead, I was a suffering person on a mission to solve the situation. I required food to reduce or recede the headache.

I entered and sat at a table ordering a Stella Artois draft, one of my favorite all-time draft beers. Downstairs they had two separate bathrooms, one had a bathroom with a urinal, the other a closed door to the commode. Unexpectantly, the commode door appeared locked or broken. I could not figure out how to gain entry inside. The waiter did not speak any English; I knew it would be impossible for me to guess out how to use the bathroom in that restaurant. Suddenly, beads of sweat developed upon my brow with the feeling like a young child who dreaded to leave class, holding it in hoping the sensation passed. I attempted going into the restroom a second time to figure it out on my own. That time I detected the door had a money slot. I returned to my table and in my best attempt at using my hands as I spoke, I asked the waiter how to operate the restroom. He made it sound like it did not require money: you only knocked if no one answered go inside. I returned for the third time, knocked, no one answered, but the door remained locked. *I do not think it will happen*, I thought. Returning upstairs to my table, I sipped the Stella draft. The entire menu was printed in French only. The positive of the menu were the pictures along with the listed prices, to figure out what I wanted to eat. With my limited budget, it restricted most of the options. I ordered a basic ham sandwich.

Upon leaving Florida. The ultimate goal of a daily budget was to spend 25 euros a day. It equated to roughly 28 dollars. The amount budgeted to cover my nightly housing and food per day for 40 days.

When the sandwich arrived, it was more like ham stuck between two pieces of hard dried bread, with no condiments on it. The only condiment available on the table was mustard, but I am not a mustard fan. I was out of luck. I consumed the dry ham sandwich the best I could as breadcrumbs fell to the table. Disastrously, the migraine worsened. I was becoming nervous because I had to return to the subway station, which would take at least 20 minutes, and then I had another half-hour train ride back to my hotel. As I sat the sweat of the discomfort intensified. My situation began deteriorating quickly. I became fearful, if I did not return to my hotel promptly, I would become sick on the train or even have an accident, like an infant.

After consuming the tasteless sandwich, I made for the door. Leaving the restaurant, the streets were full of people, numerous cars, motorcycles, and scooters—too much traffic for me. It created congestion and unnerving sounds. I contemplated, if I lived there, I would not want to drive a car. *Maybe why French citizens, mostly, appeared healthy. It was because they walked everywhere.* Then I had another thought, *Paris was not my cup of tea. I had no desire to ever return.* I knew my circumstances were probably providing me with a poor first impression. Perhaps if I had more time or with someone fluent in French, or if I spoke French myself, it would be a different trip.

Luckily, I made the journey back to my hotel room with no incidents. Though still light outside, I withdrew to bed after a much-needed restroom break. As I laid in bed, it seemed as if I was awake for two full days. I was thankful I did not become lost on the subway. I feared on the trip back the train was heading to the airport instead of my hotel location. Although I had made it, I was still disappointed. I completely could not communicate even my most basic needs to people. I utterly understood how difficult it must be when tourists and foreigners come to our country and need help or instructions. It created a mix of frustration, and fear.

Eventually, with the help of 800 mg of Advil, I drifted off to slumber. I awoke about midnight local time. The symptoms of the migraine resolved.

I still could not believe I was here in Paris. It was like I stepped into the pages of the travel adventure stories I have read. Reality blurred with fantasy. With the white sheets pulled to my chin, I could be a stowaway on a ship chugging along the Nile River or shivering at Camp Three preparing to summit Everest. Instead, only a day trip away separated me from St. Jean Pied de Port, the starting point for the pilgrimage to Santiago. A journey of the unknown.

I attempted to keep everything simple, back to basics, to remain present. My required belongings upon my back. The daily needs of food, water, along with housing were the primary goals. Secondary was to reflect, write, snap pictures, as well as savor God's beauty. I desired to be open as a child, to allow my imagination and curiosity to soar. Perhaps when I arrive at the starting point, I could recall my desires and passions in life. So far, no regrets for quitting the job, even though faced with uncertainty. I thought to myself, *I have faith, hope, and trust. I planned on taking one step at a time and remain in the present moment.*

I have a personal goal of reconnecting with myself and hopefully hear the voice inside which guides me during my Camino.

CHAPTER 7

SEPTEMBER 7TH, 2012

I departed the hotel around seven in the morning. The hotel front desk instructed me the hotel's shuttle would only take about thirty minutes to arrive at the train station, which would provide me at least two-hours before the train's departure. After an hour, the inner nerves aroused to panic as I continued to shuffle in my seat, praying the next stop would be mine. Finally, the shuttle arrived, almost one and a half hours from departure.

Upon arrival, I flew straight to the train with the printed voucher obtained back in Florida. Distressingly, it was not an actual ticket. The voucher allowed for the required ticket for boarding only once gotten from a ticket master. With about twenty minutes until departure, I sprinted up three flights of steps, with my 25-plus-pound backpack strapped along for the jaunt. I located the ticket line where at least twenty people waiting. A cloud of despair overwhelmed me. I pleaded and begged to move forward, due to my situation. Fortunately, most of the people in line spoke English and allowed me to pass. I obtained the golden ticket and jetted through the station, retracing my steps. The train's attendant punched my ticket with a smile and the train moved as both of my feet cleared the opened door. All I could think as I shuffled through the aisle, *I am blessed to be here on that train. Thank you, Lord!*

The train moved swiftly away. I cooled off and the stress of almost missing my train reduced and faded away. I prayed the next train would be a simpler undertaking. The ride was smooth as I sat backwards and observed the landscapes fly away from me at over 80 mph.

Because of being my first experience on a European train, I purchased a first-class ticket. A second reason. The ride was almost three-hours long. I wanted to experience comfort. Unfortunately, the first-class seating was not what I imagined. The seat was missing the cushioned headrest and when I went to the restroom, the water of the sink malfunctioned. However, the first-class train offered a dining car. Another bonus, the car had air condition.

Upon arrival to change trains. The wait time, over two-hours, in a humid station with nowhere to sit, except for the dirty concrete. The outside temperature reached 95-degrees Fahrenheit. My shirt stuck to my back because of the added weight and heat of my backpack, not to mention the uncomfortable sensation of boxer briefs when hot and humid. I sensed a wave of fatigue.

As I boarded the second train, even though I bought a first-class train ticket, I had to stand for two-hours shoulder to shoulder with students who had class-two tickets. It so happened it was a holiday for the local high-school students.

The highlight of the train leg, I met Mags from Ireland. She was a petite woman in her mid-twenties with shoulder-length blonde hair. A fellow single traveler who comes to find out watched *The Way* and came for the Camino. We discussed lots of subjects during the two-hour train ride. Her smile and conversation eased the discomfort of the heat and crowds.

Once I arrived at the third location to change trains for St. Jean, I realized right away I would not be having the simple transition I had hoped for. Because of the late afternoon time of arrival, the last train of the day already departed. To compensate for the error, the station charted a bus to take us to St. Jean Pied de Port.

It has been told. The journey was supposed to be the fun part, but I prayed for my destination to St. Jean.

St. Jean Pied de Port, France

CHAPTER 8

SEPTEMBER 8TH, 2012

I ultimately arrived in St. Jean around 10:30 p.m. last night. I disembarked from the bus and began searching for the check-in location. Mags, my fellow Camino pilgrim, immediately disappeared into the night. The other travelers followed suit into the black abyss. By chance, one other traveler, like me, slightly confused, remained with me. As we walked and walked, it became apparent we were lost. We stopped a local man for directions and through my companion's best broken French (hand signals were my contribution) directed ourselves to the correct location. When we reached it, it was close to 11:00 P.M. Unfortunately, all their beds were taken for the night. I was apparently beginning my Camino during the end of the busy season. They told me they had about 300 pilgrims checked-in that day. I joked, "*I should win the prize for being the last one.*" The check-in process took about thirty minutes.

They advised me about a woman who offered her home to pilgrims at the same rate as their albergue, about 10-

euros a night, and only a few blocks away. I got the directions, arrived, and knocked. The door creaked open to a frail older woman with a bright smile and welcoming kind eyes. First, she made me take my shoes off at the doorway, before entering her home. She confused me when the first room she showed me cost 30 euros. The remaining rooms were stylish, but all expensive. "*What about the ten-euro room?*" I asked. "*I was told you had them.*" She gave a little depressing sigh, showed me the laundry room with a tiny cot. "*No, I'm sorry,*" I said with a shake of my head, "*that won't work for me.*"

Instead, I thanked the woman and returned to the albergue. The door was locked, but I could hear voices inside—English voices. I knocked a little louder upon the wood and the door opened. The staff seemed surprised to see me again and allowed me back in as I told them about the price discrepancy. They apologized for the misinformation and made me an offer: since it was now nearly midnight and everything full, they would let me take a hot shower and sleep on the kitchen floor. We placed a spare twin mattress by a wall, so no one would step on me. They instructed me that people would be awake around 5 a.m. to prepare breakfast, which meant I would have to wake up. Once everyone checked out, they would help me find a place to stay that night to get quality rest before embarking on my Camino to Santiago. They advised me not to begin in the morning due to my previous 24 hours of trials. I was grateful of their advice, thanked them, and crashed the best I could. I humbly enclosed my body into my sleeping bag. Unfortunately, I only slept a few hours, mainly because my personal time clock was still on Eastern Standard Time.

As foretold, people stirred around 5 a.m. I arose and sat at the breakfast table, disheveled in appearance along with mentally fatigued, as others awoke for their morning meal. During the breakfast I observed pilgrims prepare themselves for the first day of their personal quest. They filled their stomachs on coffee, breads, jams, and cheeses. The kindness continued as the host of the albergue invited me to partake in the breakfast. I asked for a glass of milk since I did not feel like eating bread with jam and I am not a coffee drinker. She served it to me hot and in a bowl, I would normally eat cereal in. They also used those same bowls for people's coffee. Slowly, everyone made their way out on their own personal Camino. I felt left out, like being the kid not picked for a game.

Once everyone exited, the staff tried to locate a private room, so I could rest before my trip the next day. Unfortunately, everything in St. Jean was booked. "I'm sorry," he said with a shake of his head. "It is still extremely busy, with 300 to 500 pilgrims arriving each morning." After failing to find a room for me, the albergue offered to let me stay there once they had cleaned it. The normal check-in was 4:00 P.M., however, they told me I could leave my backpack there and return at 1:00 P.M. to check-in. They needed to first clean everything for the upcoming Pellegrinos, (pilgrims), or people on the Camino, who would arrive that day. *I have a bed tonight*, was my thought as I accepted the offer, and it brought a smile to my face.

After helping them put away the mattress. I changed clothes, loaded up my pockets with what I may need to cover me over the next few hours and stowed my backpack out of the way.

Departing, the narrow-cobbled streets and the architecture intrigued me. St. Jean Pied de Port offered a medieval atmosphere with a population of 1,900 people. It seemed the perfect gateway to my Camino.

My first impressions were the citizens of the town loved flowers. Everyone had gardens or planters on their windowsills. Aromas from the flowers filled the air as you strolled past.

I walked around the city snapping pictures and reading about the history. I did my best to view the major monuments. First, I visited the Bishop's Prison, a little house-like structure on the main street. The building dated back to the 14th century. It acted as a stockade during WWII.

Throughout the day, I was in awe of the archways I passed through. I located an arch, named Porte Du Roy, the king's door. It granted me access to an enormous house with views overlooking St. Jean with the Pyrenes mountains in the background.

At that time of day, the sky was absent of clouds. Only blue skies existed for my eyes. As I returned to the cobbled streets of the city, I thought it was amazing as I placed my hands-on walls which were constructed in the year 700. All the roofs of the homes and businesses were of a red tile. The masonry work standing strong though tested through the centuries. The weathered stones were of unique shapes and sizes blended together with mortar to accomplish the goals of the builder. At times during my adventure, I sensed I was passing through an old fort structure. Old walls which once protected a city against battles of knights clashing against one another.

I have only been in St. Jean the one day, but so far, I have met people from Japan, Germany, Switzerland, along with Ireland.

I paused mid-day for a vanilla ice cream cone. Because of the heat it melted instantaneously over my fingers. I experienced a temporary brain freeze attempting to beat the process. I lost. Cleaning my fingers of the sticky treat, my cell phone began falling from my pocket. As the rectangular plastic device paused in my hand, I realized it has been three days without talking on it. I was fighting the addiction of being attached to my phone. Back in Florida, my cell phone always seemed adhered to my hand or ear. I pondered how many emails I may have. *Besides, I probably should call a few people back home to inform them I was okay,* I thought. I chose not to call or check the emails. Instead, I gazed upon the phone with a roaming signal and returned it to my pocket. I knew the stripping away I desired included electronics.

As I continued through the city, I sensed a slowing of my breathing as I became relaxed. I was experiencing my true element, to feed my adventure side as well as my curiosity. I was thankful I remained in the city. It would have been a mission impossible to walk the 15-plus miles today over a mountain, with my previous days of travel.

Next, I visited a church. Inside was divine. The pews were of the old-fashioned hard-wood maple, perhaps black oak. The walls, like most structures I have viewed, built from stoned masonry. Multiple hand carved statues strategically placed throughout as the church followed a catholic theme. I lit a candle and said a prayer asking for safety on my journey. If the church was open in the morning, I may return one more time.

Outside of the church, I paused to snap a picture for two women in front of a Camino statue. The two women were from Toronto, Canada. They were best friends looking for adventure. As we shared a conversation, they mention they visited Dunedin, FL, each year to watch the Toronto Blue Jays in spring training. Since Dr. Palm Harbor, a team doctor for them, I covered their games and interacted with the players throughout the season. Possibly, we were in the stands at the same time. I would have to share this with him upon my return. I loved how the world appeared small in some regards.

I observed lots of pilgrims checking in today at surrounding albergues and hotels as I strolled through the city. It may be busy tomorrow along the way. I may not gain access to the places I desired from my readings due to them being full of pilgrims so sleeping arrangements may be more difficult than expected. Instead of fear and doubt, I continued my inner mantra, *through hope, prayer, faith, and trust; the albergues I wanted to stay in would have an open bed for me.*

After exploring the city, I returned to the albergue around 1:30 p.m. I picked a bed in the lower part of the establishment with only three other bunk beds. I entered my sleeping bag and slept a few hours before other pilgrims checked in.

Upon awaking, I unpacked my entire pack to inventory my belongings. I gazed over the stacks. I attempted again to shed an item or two to lessen my burden. Instead, I repacked. My backpack filled to capacity; I could not put another item into it. I was way over the estimated 10% of body weight advised on the Camino forums. Mine should only weigh about 14–15 pounds, I bet mine topped out at around 25–30 pounds. Internally, I was probably overweight as well. The daily grind of medicine, debt, and attempting to have a life based on what remained created a fatigue of unbearable portions.

After working on my backpack, I headed back to the streets and considered dinner. The day was still quite bright at 7:00 P.M. I roamed around reading menus, considering what to have. Not only was taste a factor but price. I decided on Italian. I sat at a table alone, however, because of the crowds, a father, and son asked to sit with me. My southern upbringing obliged. Normally, I would have remained quiet. Instead, I persisted with courage to begin a conversation. If I desired to overcome my introvert self, I required an inner transformation through baby steps. By speaking I gained a minor victory in a harmless environment. Come to find out, he was a minister, and they were walking the Camino for about a week during his son's school break. We shared a wonderful supreme pizza. After dinner, I returned to the albergue, and they departed on their way, wishing each other a Buen Camino!

Upon arrival at the albergue I returned to my sleeping area. There were three sets of bunk beds, making a capacity of six people sleeping in the same room tonight. I chose a bottom bunk. They made the bunks from metal. A three-inch mattress and one pillow provided. I covered the mattress and pillow with a sheet given to me by the host along with a blanket as well. When the other person climbed the three steps to the top bunk, or moved in any direction on their mattress, a squeaking noise ensued.

I showered, took a dose of Ambien, as well as inserted earplugs. I cuddled into my sleeping bag curling into a side-lying ball. I desired a fresh early start tomorrow. My goal was a 6:30 A.M. It would indulge my eyes to observe the sunrise. It also allowed 12 to 13 hours of daylight. I did not know my pace or possible detours to reach the destination.

My day here in St. Jean has aided me to rest and clear my mind. I finally sensed today was a positive. I fed my inner curiosity of learning and adventure and rebalanced from the chaos upon my arrival.

I decisively remembered the reason I was doing this; to feel alive, to listen to my inner voice which became faded. I prayed God guided me in my steps.

St. Jean Pied de Port, France to
Roncesvalles, Spain

CHAPTER 9

SEPTEMBER 9TH, 2012

I awoke upon my bunk before sunrise. Under the cover of a red-lighted head torch. Quietly, I gathered my belongings as others snored. I exited onto the cobbled streets saying goodbye to the albergue which was so pleasant and accommodating. I paused at the church from yesterday to light a candle asking for an open heart to the Universe. Serenely sitting on a pew, I asked God to provide me with inspiration as I headed towards a new destiny, to hear my inner voice and to live the life I have always imagined. I sensed nervous energy. I learned somewhere that nervous energy was a precursor to positive change. How many before me, including knights may have performed the same task before heading onto their own personal crusade?

As the sun arose the first glimpses of the beauty became clear to my sight. The sky offered a pink hue blended with light blues. The distant mountain peaks were grass covered. They appeared smooth, not similar to the Rocky Mountains I once viewed. The path surrounded by rolling green hills and plant-like vegetation growing over the wooden fence which ran parallel to the road. A misty fog saturated the remote low-lying regions. Overall, a stroll through the countryside.

I paused at the Refuge Orrison for lunch, a popular location for pilgrims. It offered a location to break up the Pyrenees Mountains. Though only eight kilometers (five miles) into Stage I, a smile appeared. I sensed delight I decided to drop everything for the adventure ahead of me. A handful of individuals stopped for the night. I thought about staying here myself, unfortunately, you had to make reservations far in advance. Knowing eight to ten kilometers remained, I added a few snacks to my pockets. Orrison was the last opportunity to eat until my Roncesvalles destination.

Beyond Orrison I trekked through green fields, at times filled with Manech sheep grazing. Approaching the apex, I visited the Cruz de Thibault. A stoned cross roped off filled with colorful ribbons. The cross marked the end of the paved road and the beginning of the dirt track which finished the day's travels.

Arriving in Roncesvalles, Spain, a province of Navarre, I rested upon a stone wall. A Spanish cat approached, greeting me with soft purring. Roncesvalles had a population of fifty people, in the province of Navarre, Spain. It acted as another major starting point for pilgrims who decided to avoid the trek over the Pyrenees by using some form of transportation from St. Jean de Port.

I checked into the albergue for the night, the Albergue de Peregrinos Real Colegiata de Roncesvalles. Originally established in 1127, however, had recent renovations which gave the appearance of a newer college dormitory. It had four floors of bunk beds, laundry rooms, kitchen, computer room, and a vending-machine room among other services. Each pod offered four sets of bunk beds with lockable lockers.

As I stored my belongings into the assigned locker near my bunk bed. I overheard a couple, probably in their 60s, with a recognizable country accent. Turned out, the couple were from Tupelo, Mississippi, of all places. Tupelo was approximately two-hours from my hometown. I had a cousin living there as well. How odd to meet a couple from the state I was born in! *It was funny how connected people are*, I thought to myself. We briefly shared our greetings. Afterwards, they disappeared around the corner.

I set off to locate the showers. After the day's struggles of heat, distance, and exhaustion, the steaming water provided an escape of bliss. It had to be one of the most appreciated showers of my lifetime. I probably remained under the heated water for at least twenty minutes rinsing my misery away, though I wished it could have been longer. I understood the importance of sharing, as other pilgrims were needing the same experience.

Returning to my bunk, I had time to lie supine and reflect upon the day. I walked nine hours which covered 25.1 kilometers, (15.6 miles) climbing over the Pyrenees Mountains. I began the journey at 170 meters above sea level, elevated to approximately 1,450 meters at its peak, then descended to 950 meters. I believed today's trek was the most tiresome thing I have ever done. A strenuous ordeal because of the combination of a 90-degree day, sun shining with limited clouds, coupled with the steep climbs and descents. It seemed the climbing would never end. However, descending the mountain deemed harder because of trying to stop my momentum and not falling on the loose rocks. The brutal heat led to many water refill opportunities to be dry. Throughout the trek, were locations to refill water bottles. Some were stone statues others were fountains you found in a local school or airport. Though I drank about a gallon of water, I easily required another gallon to quench my thirst.

I walked baby steps at numerous times. I used my trekking poles for stability. The poles are a must. They assisted with balance especially when going downhill and removed pressure from my knees. Many other pilgrims lapped my pace. I stopped at a mountain shelter which could be used in an emergency if the weather became harsh. Relinquishing the weighty backpack, I ate upon the snacks I purchased earlier in the day. The backpack was burdensome. My shoulders ached already. I knew I needed to find a way to drop some weight. I decided I would walk one more day, if the weight continued to pull on my shoulders, I would either mail items home or donate items to other pilgrims.

The original goal was to journal on my breaks. I thought it would be the easiest way to capture my present moments or scribble observations. The plan conceived too difficult to journal during the day. My breaks were brief, primarily used to sip water or pause to remove the weight of my pack upon my shoulders. Second, for laziness. I had to remove my pack, open it to get the journal, then write.

Once completed, reverse the steps to begin again. Instead, I remained in the present moment, to focus on my steps, the surrounding beauty, along with the sounds I heard. I thought once I arrived at my day's destination, I could reflect and write about the day's ordeals, adventures, and thoughts.

My overweight backpack aside, the walk was peaceful. Sounds of traffic, cell phones, among other nuisances vanished into an orchestra of natural sounds from birds and the local sheep population. The views were stunning. My mind did not race too much as I focused on my steps. I sensed I entered a bubble. The world around me disappeared. It was solely left, right, left, right. No worries about debt, chaos in change, or what others may be thinking. I sensed purity, innocence, almost childlike. I followed as much of the natural paths as possible instead of the easier paths by the major asphalt road.

From my understanding, today's heat was rare. Most of the time, cooler temperatures with the constant threat of thunderstorms or worse in crossing those mountains occurred. In the movie, *The Way*, today's section was where Emilio Estevez's character perished because of the severe weather.

Closing the hard-covered journal, I cracked open the guidebook. I read about tomorrow's stage. A major advantage of using John Brierley's *A Pilgrim's Guide to the Camino de Santiago*, the wealth of information he provided. Besides the map and key locations, it added to the adventure by describing the history as well as inspirational comments to guide the pilgrim along the path.

With 7:00 P.M. approaching, I exited the top bunk to attend mass. The mass provided a blessing of safety during your pilgrimage. They held it in the nearby Iglesias de Santa Maria. Entering through an arched doorway, I choose to sit in the back of the church, on a few concrete steps. Because I am not Catholic, I considered myself a non-denominational Christian, I did not want to interfere with their ceremony. The positive of my viewpoint, the steps allowed me to gaze upon the parade of priests and bishops dressed in their Catholic attire entering. They were chanting in Latin as they continued towards the altar. Leading up to the present moment, I had not attended church regularly in twelve years. I was under the self-belief that no matter where I stood, I considered that church, especially when in nature. I believed in God and have read the Bible before. I trusted in prayer along with faith. I have attended a Catholic service once when a friend of mine invited me to a midnight mass. Though I did not understand the words, the ritual was interesting to watch. The organ music played promoted a soothing and lovely environment. The priest offered a special blessing for us pilgrims no matter our faith. When time approached for their communion, I said a thank you under my breath and departed.

The pilgrim's meal began at 8:00 P.M. At first, I considered not attending due to attempting to save money. The meal itself costs 10-euros. I planned to make a sandwich or eat anything I could locate in the vending machines. On the other hand, I was famished as my stomach growled and howled. It was worth spending 10-euros for a hot meal to replenish today's journey. Additionally, I decided since it was my first night, I should relish in the company of others. Part of the pilgrimage experience was to interact. I am predominantly an introvert. I rarely interacted with others besides people at work or my recent girlfriend. The experience of the Camino created an opportunity to step out of my comfort zone, to push my boundaries. Besides, the dinner itself offered a sheltered environment. I would not be rejected or told to sit somewhere else.

The pilgrim's dinner was amazing. Not only was the food tantalizing to the taste buds. The setup allowed communion and fellowship easily as 8–10 people sat around a circular wooden table. We had pasta with a fired spicy sausage as our first course, then trout with French fries as the second with vanilla ice cream to complete the meal. The 10-euro meal also covered the provided bottle of local red wine. I drank a glass and greatly savored it. I have never appreciated wine in the past, but that local one had a unique, and enjoyable taste. The company I met was a blessing. It introduced me to fellow pilgrims from New Zealand, Oregon, and England. Ultimately, the meal and conversation lasted about forty-five minutes. It was a pleasant experience to be part of toasts, surrounded by others sharing a meal, and laughing. Though finally, my inner battery weakened. I required some personal recharge through solitude, not to mention the food coma. I politely said goodnight and exited the restaurant.

Unfortunately, returning to the albergue, about ten minutes after my meal, a curtain of nausea overcame me. The sensation hit me quickly, without warning. Luckily, to my left, a public restroom in a building outside which offered discretion. I vomited the entire meal through multiple heaves. Maybe due to the over exertion from today's walk or I ate too much too quick. Instantly afterwards, I appeared fine with no further problems or issues. I returned to my bunk.

As I continued with deep breaths sensing the Ambien dreams approaching, I was glad I was secure, warm, as well as comfortable. I smiled knowing some thought I was mad for my decision to leave Florida.

I told myself I would continue to converse with the Angels. I believed they were overlooking my wellbeing. Eventually, I believed I could hear something from my heart. My heart would be a channel for some higher wisdom. I had faith I would receive an answer.

Roncesvalles To Larrasoana

CHAPTER 10

SEPTEMBER 10TH, 2012

A difficult last night for me, I only slept from 10:00 P.M. to 10:45 P.M. and midnight to 2:30 A.M. even with the assistance of Ambien and ear plugs. The remainder of the night I tossed and turned oddly after such a strenuous Stage I. It was my first experience spending the night in such a large albergue. The albergue had four floors, an overall count of 730-plus pilgrims trying to sleep. Imagine, throughout the night people were snoring, getting up for the bathroom, or talking in their sleep.

With crusted eyes, my watch displayed 6:30 A.M., I disembarked from the top bunk to gather my belongings. Today's walk, 27.4 kilometers, (roughly 17 miles). The ultimate destination was Larrasoana. I began the trek at 7:30 A.M. My backpack seemed lighter even though I did not lessen the weight load. Maybe my pack pretended to be lighter due to the high dosage of Advil. It repaired the damage to my body from the first day, so the backpack did not create the shoulder pain as it did yesterday. Or it was a fresh day, I was on an adventure, and knew my curious eyes were observing unfamiliar landscapes I have never seen before. It created excitement to place one foot in front of the other.

Shortly after my departure, a few hikers paused at the Santiago de Compostela sign. I snapped the classic picture next to it, displaying 790 kilometers (491 miles) to reach Santiago. The distance at hand caused my insides to become queasy; an alarming force conquered my body. Four-hundred-ninety-one miles, plus more possibly. I never walked over five miles until yesterday. I inhaled a deep breath, gazed forward, and took a step.

Today's walk, mostly wooded paths under blue skies, alongside running streams, and a slight breeze created a wonderful day. The country was beautiful. Along the way one would observe historical structures hidden along the forest route, churches among the towns, as well as the majestic landscapes. It reminded me of the path to grandmother's house in a fairy tale. It made me crave the butter beans, black eye peas, fried okra, cornbread, and green beans my Granny Ray would cook. *I was a country boy on the Camino*, I laughed.

About three-hours into today's trek my shoulders ached again. The weight of the backpack creating discomfort. No matter how I attempting to adjust the padded straps the pain continued. I sensed a hot spot developing on my left foot. A rubbing raw sensation—my first possible blister. I paused and removed the thin athletic socks and replaced them with thicker wool socks for added cushion and protection. After lacing up the trekking shoes I continued along the path. Though hurting I told myself, *I was the one who chose to walk this path.*

I finally hit a wall around 1:00 P.M. My shoulders had a constant ache. If I could, I would have stopped right there for the evening. Dejectedly, about three-and-a-half hours remained to Zubria, with another five-and-a-half kilometers (three-plus miles) from Larrasoana. I filled the remaining hours with small steps and many breaks.

Upon arrival in Larrasoana. I could not stay where I planned on, the albergue was full. A penalty of my slower pace along with the number of pilgrims still beginning their journey. Instead, the albergue I had to choose offered horrible accommodations. A coed room filled with bunk beds with no air-conditioning. I assumed the heat would create a tough sleeping environment. They asked me to sleep on a top bunk, not my preferred location. The bathroom had an open four shower-head shower system, similar to the ones back in a high-school locker room. One for the women and another for the men, with icy water only. It possessed two-bathroom stalls. Limited resources for over 100 pilgrims.

After completing a cold shower and stowing my belongings on the bunk, I decided to locate food. Down the street about three blocks away, a little café offered a plate of chicken and rice at a reasonable price. I consumed the tasty meal leaving only a spotless plate because of my hunger. After I ate, I strolled around Larrasoana. I detected symbols and armorial shields on the stone buildings which were exceptional. They built the buildings in the 10th century.

Upon return to the albergue, I met a gentleman from India who shared in a similar situation in life which I did. He was a physician, but desired more from his existence. He knew life offered more than what his daily routine suggested. We clicked well together. He was a few years older than me. He asked how things were so far. Besides the beauty and my personal desires, I mentioned my backpack. He offered to assist and went through the backpack to help me lighten it with a thorough shakedown. He held each item and asked if it was a true essential or a want. I tried to be honest with myself and him, though saying goodbye to an object deemed more difficult than I imagined. In the end, I donated about five pounds of gear, or approximately $300 worth, but well worth it. In reality, I should have dropped more. I contemplated mailing it back home for later use; instead, I donated the supplies to the Pilgrim's box. May it help someone else. My backpack seemed much lighter. I began learning I did not need much stuff. A lesson for the internal life as well. My backpack improved its fit with the reduction of weight and supplies. I even found two new straps which made it fit to my body better too. Each day a new lesson learnt.

As the sun began to set, I attempted to lie in the bunk surrounded by 99 other pilgrims. The heat adding to the difficult surroundings. My body was sticking to the internal sleeping bag material. I had to remove myself and lie on their sheet.

As the minutes clicked away before sacking out, I promised myself one major thing, *savor it. The goal was to live each day to its fullest. I am an explorer. I was seeing lands for the first time. As a predominant introvert I should use the experience to interact with unknown people.*

Looking back, I should have covered less ground in that early Stage II. Day one was a stretch to complete it all, a grueling introduction to the Camino. On day two I could have reduced my miles to protect my body. It has always been told that the beginning stages of a long trek were the point where a hiker was most prone to injuries. I should have used those first few days or longer as an adaptation phase. Do not become a casualty in the first two weeks or less because you were eager to reach a destination.

Larrasoana To Pamplona

CHAPTER 11

SEPTEMBER 11TH, 2012

I arose early, after a troublesome night's sleep. The numerous pilgrims snoring and moving around on their bunks in the crowded open room only allowed four hours of sleep with a lot of tossing and turning. I surrendered and decided on an early start for my journey.

Upon departure, the sky was lightless. I switched on my headlamp to follow the path and ensure I located the yellow guiding arrows of the Camino. Limited with tunnel vision, the surroundings provided calmness as I walked next to the Rio Arga.

As the moments of solitude progressed, the horizon developed into a saturated sky, consumed with crimson, suddenly the sun surfaced. I saw God in the sunrise. Finally, I had a glimpse of living in the moment. Instantly, the failures of the past along with the fears of the future disappeared. My breath softened as I paused at the splendid appearance. I gazed upon the colors as an innocent child. I was pure. A warmth overtook my soul; I was living out my dream.

I continued under blue skies with minimal cloud coverage. The pace sustained; I became sluggish around five hours of walking. My mind drifted. My steps reminding me when I was back in Florida, I was not happy or fulfilled. I understood I had to take accountability for myself to overcome those obstacles. It was up to me to seek an alternative pathway. I knew whatever choice I made; difficulties would emerge. People thought I was mad. They were crabs in the bucket stating how I should be at work today, instead of on that dusty dirt path in Spain. I believed I required a touch of madness. It demanded acts like mine to take the next step in obtaining your dreams. The potentiality of dreams coming true which made life interesting.

I failed to reach the guidebook's stage end of Cizur Menor. My fatigued body with aching shoulders paused my forward progression. Instead, I stopped and remained in Pamplona. I sensed the mild anxiety of defeat. I had always been strict on myself to complete whatever task I preset myself, almost like a machine or robot. I used it as a maturing moment. To learn to leap from my comfort zone and not always go by the rule book. To allow myself to fail without inner self-negative chatter.

I detected the increase of noise as I closed in on Pamplona, a major city. It had a populace of around 190,000 people, whereas Larrasoana, from the night before, had a community of about 200. They considered Pamplona the capital of the Navarre province. The most popular event of Pamplona festivals each year, the Running of the Bulls or the Feast of San Fermin. A major bonus of stopping here for the evening were the Gothic-style churches. Pamplona appealed as a stunning city. It possessed side streets filled with bars, open plazas, and shops.

As the routine unfolded upon arrival, I checked into an albergue and chose a bed. I washed my clothes by hand, hung them to dry, and took a shower, then, sightsaw. It may seem odd of instead of sitting or relaxing, after walking over 18 kilometers (11.1 miles), I could not wait to walk more. I wanted to visualize the history along with the sights of an unknown city. Most pilgrims I saw upon their check-in, moseyed straight for a nap or a rest from the day's exhaustion.

I ran into my friend from India, we located a small pub sharing a beer and conversation. As our glasses toasted, we smiled knowing we were currently in control of our lives and not being controlled by fate or another person. He shared how medicine in India created a brutal existence for him. He talked about the long hours with the lack of basic supplies. The combination had him questioning his future. He struggled with the decision, as I did. In theory, we were creating a wealthy lifestyle compared to many. We acknowledged gratefulness, yet unfilled. The pilgrimage acted as an avenue to take responsibility and choose a different pathway. I mentioned the inner struggle of remaining on the hamster wheel or following the love to travel. We agreed we were on a journey to accomplish a higher life. Him and I continued sipping our ale filled pints knowing everything was possible. We admitted we were not timid to dream, and to yearn for everything we would like to see happen in our life. The last sip taken, we shook hands and departed company.

Afterwards, I walked through the city until I entered the Plaza del Castillo. The plaza saturated with restaurants, businesses, and large numbers of people. I chose an out-door restaurant even though the evening air remained hot. From where I sat, I observed the plaza. I watched children playing with balloons, street performers off in the distance acting like statues, along with couples' hand in hand. I enjoyed a dinner of chicken, rice, and a Stella draft. Suddenly, once again upon the completion of my meal, I immediately vomited it all up. Thankfully, they had an empty open restroom. *Maybe I was eating too much at one sitting, perhaps too fast, or a combination of the two,* I wondered. After I vomited; no symptoms remained. I became concerned. It was the second episode. The anxiety rose, and I wondered if it would continue or if I was under the influence of a disease, which may cause those symptoms.

I continued around the city after the episode with dinner. I came across the coolest statue I had seen so far. The statue depicted the celebration of the running of the bulls. Sculpted from a hard-silver metal. The marvelously crafted bulls standing side by side appeared in motion. I sensed I should move to avoid penetration from their sharpened horns. Unfortunately, the camera battery had no life. Though no picture snapped, I had it in my mind forever.

Though a remarkable city, I wanted a return to nature which offered serenity. After completing a few hours of sightseeing, I returned to the albergue. I crawled into my sleeping bag to a night of rest inviting a fresh tomorrow. As I closed my eyes, I sent up a silent prayer, *A brand-new day tomorrow: may my feet toughen, and my physical strength grow as I continued my path.*

Excitement remained. It was easy to cultivate a positive outlook. Each day I saw something new. Like a child, I remained in a state of awe. A state I desired to maintain each day moving forward.

Pamplona To Puente de la Reina

CHAPTER 12

SEPTEMBER 12TH, 2012

The sun barely upon the horizon. My exposed arms produced goosebumps from the chill. I considered putting on my fleece. Instead, I knew it would warm up as the sun continued to rise. I trudged through the slight crispness. Thoughts of Pamplona swirled in my head as I made my way toward Puente de la Reina.

I shared the morning for two-hours with two gentlemen from Italy and New Jersey. Those interactions usually began with "Buen Camino." Then based on walking pace, the interaction may be brief or, like that morning, a couple of hours. Normally, the walking was in silence except for the sounds of rubber soles upon the dusty earth. Occasionally, you may intervene with asking their home location, how their trek was progressing, or the day's destination. The interaction provided comfort and confidence, as well as much needed support based on the inner conflicts or feelings a pilgrim may be experiencing.

The landscape to Puente de la Reina normally journeyed through bountiful cereal lands. Yet, in September
they are harvested-earth wastelands. I imagined the fields
covered in colors instead of brown dirt. It would have made
a perfect scene for an artist's painting, prime for any gal-
lery in the world. I enjoyed the soil paths instead of asphalt
or concrete, it reminded me of the red clay earth of Zama,
Mississippi. From our front porch, dirt roads led out of
town or up to the school, church, and cemetery. I recalled
being a young child running across them or playing with
toys. The time of innocence and imagination.

As the day's journey continued, I could see something
of my soul in the plants and birds of the fields. Slowly becoming free and undergoing a nourishing growth. Each
stone today was welcoming. They marked those stones with
the recognizable yellow arrow of the Camino. As I approached each one, an inner thrill arose as I knew I was
one step closer to St. James. I passed through a section of
wind turbines. The views from the overlooking mountains
off in the distance were superb.

Before entering Puente de la Reina, I detoured to
Eunate. The primary reason for the detour, I desired to
visit the Eunate church. Built in the 12th century, they considered it a jewel of the Camino. They dedicated the
Eunate Church to the Virgin Mary and one of the only two
octagon churches in Spain.

As I approached the Church of Saint Mary of Eunate, I
watched a man shepherding in a vast field. As I walked
through and around the church, I attempted to count the
arches. I read it had 33 in total. The isolated location offered

a peaceful atmosphere. I pondered the hundreds of thousands of previous pilgrims who have visited those stone walls. I strolled around the outside and inside, marveling at its beauty. I wanted to light a candle and say a prayer, but they only had electronic ones. I sat on a wooden pew which creaked under my body weight pausing to allow my spiritual energy to renew. I had faith in my path and the decision I had made.

I departed as a slight drizzle fell from the skies. With the wind becoming strong, I thought, *Time to go.* I continued—the common theme. I had almost four-and-a-half kilometers (almost three miles) to Puente de la Reina.

The city of Puente de la Reina, deemed the "Bridge of the Queen." The bridge considered an example of Romanesque architecture. When researching the Camino, I discovered it was one of the most frequently photographed bridges along the route.

As I crossed the bridge, I pondered how I have always loved bridges. Was it the power of the water beneath? Was it the connection of two lands? Did the bridge act as a physical wonder which fed my curiosity based on their construction? Or have bridges always sparked a spiritual meaning? Hard to say, perhaps all of those. I just know when I crossed a bridge, I sensed peace, joy, and wonder.

I stopped at the Albergue Jakue. Located near an amazing pilgrim's monument, it offered multiple comforts, compared to most of the albergues. Once inside, I saw it possessed a common room which had comfortable sofas for relaxing, reading books, or writing. Out back, an outdoor patio with gorgeous views as bonus. If I truly desired to splurge, they offered massages and private rooms, but I stuck to my 25-euros-a-day policy.

After checking in, I washed and dried my clothes in a machine. Laundry using a machine seemed like a reward rather than a chore. I went halves with another pilgrim, named Michael. It allowed both of us to save a few euros. He was from Germany. It turned out I met him in St. Jean on my first night when I had to sleep on the floor. He sat at the breakfast table that morning, departing just a day before me.

I escaped to my bunk to lie down around 7:00 p.m. I perceived the exhaustion catching up to me. Though amazed after 13 miles, approximately 7 hours, I could not sleep. Once in my bunk, my body ached, however my mind danced awake. Images of the day, or pondering the next move consumed my thoughts. Though I tried to remain present, thoughts of the future were seeping in. I guess another Ambien night with ear plugs.

Curled in the sleeping bag, I thought of how I rejoiced my alone time, as others walked in groups of two or even six.

I recalled a quote, "I love to be alone. I never found the companion that was so companionable as solitude."
—Henry David Thoreau.

I just focused on my steps. Perhaps it was my technique for living in the moment. I was thankful for the abundance which appeared today, encountering fresh grapes on the vines which were used to make the local wine, ripe red tomatoes, and corn on the stalk. I almost picked a few for my dinner tonight. It prompted me how bountiful our world was. Even though at times I may see scarcity, our world provided plentiful resources. As the fruit flourished, it reminded me I was growing anew. I departed the daily grind I disliked. I was like a new seed pushing through its covered barrier, reaching for the energy of the sun, desiring to taste the rain.

Puente de la Reina To Estella

SEPTEMBER 13TH, 2012

I awoke with 685 kilometers (425.6 miles) to Santiago de Compostela. Today's walk destined for Estella with a distance of about 21.9 kilometers (13.6 miles). The stage promised natural paths instead of along major roads with cars buzzing by. I yearned for the open fields with olive trees and vineyards promised by the guidebook.

I departed from the albergue into darkness. The primary illumination from the streetlights, lining the path through the city. I relished the peaceful nature and the silence. As the sun rose upon the distant horizon, the sky radiated a pink tint. The harvested fields maintained their brown monotony; however, the vineyards added a greenish hue of life to the landscape.

Storm clouds surrounded me in the afternoon. It began misting. I thought I may have my first true rainstorm. For protection, I unpacked and dressed in my rain gear, but then the sun came out almost immediately. As the sun pierced through the clouds, I removed the rain gear and replaced it into my backpack. However, like a cruel joke, it misted again. Because I chose not to purchase a plain pull-over poncho, every time it rained, I had to shed my backpack, retrieve my rain gear, dress, apply the backpack rain cover, then put my backpack back on. A lot of work to say the least. To top it off, the rain gear intensified the heat. The second time around, I simply embraced the mist with an underlying prayer for it to dissipate.

Blissfully, another day filled with meeting people along my path. I met new individuals from Holland and Australia. With a "Buen Camino," I reconnected with the two Canadians today. I personally enjoyed going a couple days without seeing someone and then suddenly seeing them again. It was like coming home for the holidays or seeing that friend you grew up with. The interaction provided comfort knowing the person was well and maintaining their path. My introvert self-understanding the importance of friendship and family. We, as pilgrims, looked out for each other. Here were multiple stars from around the world intertwining, creating their own universe. All moving in crazy orbits, yet all moving toward one goal—St. James in Santiago.

As I walked, mostly my mind remained blank. I looked down at the surface, listening to my trekking poles' tips alternate with my rubber-soled shoes. At times, out of left field, thoughts flooded my thinking. *I wished I were pain free and stronger. What if I trekked a bit farther than a stage? Perhaps by doing so, there would be more open beds available.* The Camino was still populated. I continued to have mild anxiety no beds would be available when I entered a terminus town.

With no beds I would have to camp out, get a private hotel, or continue into the darkness of night until the next albergue. Those thoughts did not increase my speed. It seemed I had maxed out at two miles per hour. I quickly fought those thoughts off, like a Mike Tyson uppercut, and returned to the present moment. My favorite tactic employed, pause and gaze at the 360-degree beauty of the Camino de Santiago. I learned to spin my neck backwards to see where I came from. Otherwise, tunnel vision developed only allowing yourself to look straight ahead or down at your own feet.

A fear since day one was contracting something like scabies or bedbugs from the crowded albergues. The fear shared by many trekkers. They warned prospective pilgrims on the forums bed bugs are present all along the Camino. Imagine over 300-hundred additional people daily, over a four-month time frame, coming from all over the world. Everyone sharing beds, chairs, showers, etc. The albergues do their best to ensure everything was clean for the next group, but bedbugs still occurred. Alarmingly, I began itching in my groin along today's trek. I had faith it was a simple rash, perhaps because of chaffing or the heat. I prayed not anything dreadful like scabies or bed bug bites. At some point, a self-inspection was required.

Upon arrival in Estella. The albergue I chose had a distance of a one-and-a-half-kilometer climb above the city, away from the attractions. Once checked in, I chose not to explore Estella or its churches. I decided I did not want to return to the city. Instead, after unpacking a few items I sat at a table in the Estella albergue, listening to English classical music allowing my body and mind to relax. I choose not to push myself, instead I breathed in joy of the Camino. Sitting quietly until 7:00 p.m., I retired to my bed. The twin bed at the albergue was not the greatest, but at least it was not a bunk bed or, better yet, a hot-sticky top bunk. The mattress had a large oval yellow repugnant stain, and I do not trust the pillows. Suddenly, I wished to either leave in the darkness or I was on a clean-sheeted top bunk. I applied their sheets over the mattress, along with the pillowcases. I had to place one pillow under the mattress where a piece of wood was broken, to act as a stabilizer. The mattress sagged from right to left. I wanted to avoid rolling onto the floor or being stuck in one position all night.

Lying inside the protection of my sleeping bag, my stomach grumbled. I hoped I was replenishing enough calories; I have not eaten any large meals recently. I was nervous of the vomiting episodes and aware of my strict 25-euro-a-day budget. It was too early to see any weight or strength losses. To maintain a positive outlook on my limited food intake and my pilgrimage I related it to Jesus' fasting on his journey to Mount Sinai. Both were 40 days. He went to Mount Sinai and I on a quest for St. James in Santiago, then onward to Finisterra and Muxia. We were both undertaking a transfiguration. Jesus bridged between Heaven and Earth as I bridged my past to my future.

I continued to debate my future. I pondered if I should return to be a practicing physician assistant. Overall, I had almost 15 years of orthopedic experience, 13 as a certified athletic trainer, and the past three as a physician assistant with Dr. Palm Harbor. In the past three years, I learned so much about the shoulder, elbow, as well as the knee—including complicated surgical techniques. I prepped the patient, understood the proper anatomy, and placing of anchors, plates, and screws. On the other hand, perhaps something else was my calling. Hopefully, God lets me know His plan. *For I can do everything through Christ, who gives me strength.*

Estella To Torres del Rio

CHAPTER 14

SEPTEMBER 14TH, 2012

I awoke around 4:30 a.m. I continued to have difficulty sleeping and only remained asleep around 4–5 hours per night. Even with ear plugs and Ambien, I disturbed easily by the snoring or rustling in bunks by the other pilgrims. The cycle brewed an inner fatigue.

While packing I saw my first bed bug. While wearing my head torch to not disturb the other sleepers. The red light illuminated the single bed bug. It appeared as if he watched me pack and was sad at my departure. Hopefully, I escaped unharmed and none of his friends were in my belongings. I searched around and saw no others. Perhaps he acted as the scout. If I stayed, he would have called in the cavalry to attack me.

Upon departure, I walked in darkness and silence once again. I was the first to exit from the albergue. The plan today had a destination to Los Arcos, about 21.1 kilometers (13.1 miles). Today's walk, another day predominately filled with natural paths through meadows, olive trees, and desert areas.

Shortly into my early start, I drank from the famous Bodegas Irache wine fountain, Fuente de Vino. They designed it as a knight's shield. Dismally, the red wine tasted bitter, I spit out the first sip.

As the sun rose, I paused overlooking a barren landscape which revealed mountain ranges. The sky was clear with a magnificent pink aura to the east. Suddenly, a breeze picked up. I imagined I could see Santiago in the distance. Was there a treasure there for me? Was there an inner voice to guide me once I arrived? I believed the answer screamed yes. Cherishing gratefulness, it blessed me to be looking into the unknown and thankful I was free as the wind. I believed nothing held me back, except myself. I trusted those steps along the way. I was once told, *"God prepares a path for everyone to follow."*

I pushed on most of the day completely alone, focused on the rhythm of my steps. The beat I created reminded me of my six-stringed guitar at home. I missed hearing the strums daily.

So far, I had no breakthrough realizations about my future. It concerned me nothing minor or even major has occurred. I promised myself patience. However, doubt seeded since I sacrificed many aspects of my life to reach a new understanding. Perhaps, it was impossible to foresee everything.

A wonderful accomplishment today, I have visited and prayed in the only two octagon churches in Spain. Today I visited the Church of the Holy Sepulchre in Torres del Rio

(Navarra), built in the 12th century. "An enigmatic building, the most singular Romanesque temples on the Road to Santiago," according to the internet. The Church nowadays, considered a funeral church along the route to Santiago. Constructed with a single-octagonal floor and finished with an eight-sided lantern. The crucifix presided over the temple with a real crown and four nails.

With my eyes closed, thoughts unwound. I established what I could truly rely on: faith, hope, and love. I had complete confidence in myself and God, as well as trusted I could rely on Him to watch over me as I walked upon the journey. Faith allowed me to maintain my optimistic outlook that all shall be well and whatever happened in my future shall place me improved from my past. Though I may not have it now, I had confidence to have it in my future. My hope provided me the feeling of expectation. I trusted my dreams shall become reality. I sensed agape love, unconditional love. With those three things, I had no hesitation to pursue my burning desire for the life I always wanted to live.

Torres del Rio To Logrono

CHAPTER 15

SEPTEMBER 15TH, 2012

A predawn start, I began by 5:30 a.m. As I walked through the darkness, with my head torch providing the illumination to keep a keen eye for my yellow arrows, a thought creeped into my mind. By leaving before the sunrise, I missed observing various marvels the pilgrimage provided. It reminded me of working those long hours. I was limiting what I observed. It forged not having a balanced life. Like that morning, I approached a small ancient structure with an opened door. They could have built it in the early centuries of man, yet I had no clue. Because of the darkness, I could not explore its treasures. Instead, it appeared only as a rock structured mound. I passed on with regret and slightly down cast.

The walk to Logano, mostly on natural paths, which were my favorite. Passing through harvested fields with geometric plots of vineyards with dark flourishing green vines of red grapes filled my hours. A highlight of the day was the Ebro River. The flowing water produced natural sounds which soothed the soul during the stage. I believed water represented life, an essential to our survival. It acted as a healing potion to purify the spirit. It provided endless inspiration.

Logano, established in the Rioja region, well known for the best wines in Spain. The trek today endured almost 20 kilometers (12.4 miles). The city had a population of 152,000 people, another colossal city. It so happened when I arrived, the festival of San Mateo was being celebrated.

I desired to stay in a certain albergue highly recommended from online forum research, but it was closed for the festival. The albergue I stayed in cost three extra euros for the same facilities, but with fewer beds. I stood in a line to check-in, praying the beds were not all taken. Happily, a bed was awarded. An added benefit of the location, it had a pool of cool water to submerge your feet in to allow them to soothe. The water was chilly, but pleasant after walking all of those miles. It provided a renewal for my aching feet.

A theme arose as I looked upon the surrounding pilgrims at the albergue, even though I departed early each morning—usually one of the first out the door, I waited in line with the same people in the albergues each night. Awaiting in those lines brought on anxiety along with fear. Plus, the darkened morning exits caused me to be missing out on beautiful scenery. I questioned why I was leaving early in the first place: *Maybe it was not worth it.*

Once I checked into my bunk and performed my normal duties, I sightsaw. I searched for a grocery store to obtain food. It appeared the entire population packed into the streets partying. The festival of San Manteo resembled a wild and crazy spring break I used to experience in Daytona Beach Florida. I saw drinking, vomiting, peeing in the streets—from guys and girls, kissing and singing. All ages were drinking and partying. The clubs all blasting techno music penetrating the streets. I spoke with a local girl and even snapped my picture with her. She was learning English and wanted to have a conversation to not only hear my dialect, but to see if she could carry on a conversation with me. I should have stayed and partied with them as she asked. Instead, I returned to my albergue. The inner true introvert won the battle. A stunning local girl asked me to remain, though my thoughts were to return to the albergue alone.

I have walked seven days. The routine coming along: I awake, walk, check into an albergue, shower, hand wash my clothes, go sightseeing, cook dinner, and go to bed. I withdrew to sleep when most were leaving for dinner and drinking.

Lying curled in the sleeping bag, I thought how the concept of my pilgrimage was irrational. Boldly, I believed it was the exit I craved to slingshot me from my unhappy daily grind. I declared I was an independent soul. I shall continue to ensure I would do what was best for me along the journey. Though what was best for me may actually not be the easiest option. I believed I was on the correct pathway. I have proven I can do whatever I focus my mind to. Like Nike, "just do it" was the new formula.

Logrono to Azofra

CHAPTER 16

SEPTEMBER 16TH, 2012

Last night, sack time occurred by 6:00 p.m. The combination of walking all day, followed by sightseeing, topped off with Ambien and ear plugs equaled lights out. Upon awaking, fellow pilgrims told me the city had an extravagant fireworks display around midnight, which were thundering and impressive. I did not hear one pop or bang.

I departed at 5:45 a.m., either Ventosa or Najera—depending on my mood and strength, was the planned destination. The first observation along the darkened streets, were people still partying. It appeared I missed out on a possible once-in-a-lifetime experience. Sometimes an introvert personality removes you from the present moment. As I stepped across the concrete, a tinge of regret threatened to overwhelm me. Yet, I let it go and continued my steps moving forward.

The morning trek, primarily alongside the boisterous highway, instead of my favorite natural peaceful paths. About two-hours into walking, my left knee induced unrelenting pain. No injury I was aware of had occurred, like a twist or hyperextension. It was the second time the searing pain overtook me. The first, during a descent of a loose rock path a few days ago. My pace slowed to a turtle's. I almost had to stop at my current spot and sit down. Instead, I pushed through until I reached Ventosa, a small hamlet in La Rioja, Spain. The population calculated at 166 people.

I located a café and sat outside. I thought I may have to stop and remain overnight there because of the extreme pain. The concern my pilgrimage was over crossed my mind instantly. I immediately prayed silently for healing, hoping, as well as begged the pain would diminish. I massaged the inside and outside of my knee as I grabbed another chair to elevate it. Periodically I stood, though the pain cut into me to the point I had no choice but to sit back down rapidly. It froze me. I wondered if I damaged my meniscus, an inner piece of cartilage in the knee. From my experience in Orthopedics patients with a meniscus tear described the exact pain I had. The injury usually led to surgery. However, I do not recall any mechanism of trauma except the daily grind of trekking. From time to time, I meditated with positive affirmations I was okay and pain free. I trusted I could force the pain away and heal myself. I believed with the power of the mind I could overcome any consequence with positive, optimistic thoughts. Though it would have been nice if Jesus could have touched my knee at that very moment. I recalled a Bible story a time Jesus healed a man based on the faith alone of another. I continued to sit quietly.

After an hour break, the throbbing present, I began again. My desire to complete the day's stage was stronger than the thought of stopping for the day. I willed myself forward. I attempted anything I could to ease the pain, including switching the guidebook to my right pocket. Focusing on my steps and leaning heavily on my trekking poles for support, eventually, through the Lord's blessing, the pain vanished after about an hour of walking. I was relieved and filled with joy.

Later on, as I approached Najera, they were setting up a stage for some Festival. Najera seemed like another alluring, historic town. I stopped at an albergue, but a sign on the door stated full—no vacant beds. That was the negatives of a slow pace or a day of injury during the busy season of the Camino. I contemplated a plan: either splurge and purchase a hotel or keep walking to the next major town, Azofra, almost another six kilometers. I grabbed a snack and sat by the water to rest, relax and ponder.

After the break, my knee remained pain free, and I had a renewed spirit of energy. I began the trek to Azofra. Outside of the city the path transitioned to country tracks passing through farmlands.

Upon arrival in Azofra, the guidebook recommended the Albergue Municipal. Elation arose because, although 180 people could stay there, it had only two beds per cubicle. Perhaps a quiet, restful sleep was possible tonight. It also had a lovely outside patio. Unfortunately, it was full. The host pushed me into an overflow area down the street with four others. The building contained a kitchen with a picnic style table and a hallway of rooms similar to a college dormitory. So, instead of intimate cubicles and two beds, I had to share a room with three other people—but at least the beds were singles and not bunk beds. Though I wished we could have had our own rooms, especially since it was only us there. I guess the owner may have been expecting others to arrive as the evening progressed.

Up to the point of arrival, I had only spent eight euros on the day, so I went into town to have a full sit-down dinner. Azofra strikes one as a friendly village, with a population under 500 people. Dinner cost seven euros. It was well worth it, as fatigue spawned no desire to cook.

The menu I abided by most days contained: a breakfast of two donuts, a power bar, a piece of fruit, and a small Coke; the snacks and lunch were usually another energy bar, an added piece of fruit, along with slices of turkey deli meat rolled up—I tried Nutella but not a big fan of it; for dinner, I either prepared pasta with sauce or dined on a sandwich. When hungry beyond those means or too exhausted to prepare dinner, I splurged on the Pilgrim's meal which normally cost 10-euros.

Upon return from dinner with a filled stomach, I turned in early—as always. Lying supine inside my sleeping bag, I pondered the future of my Camino. Per the guidebook, I needed six days to complete the loop of Finisterra and Muxia. I then caught a bus back to Santiago. I thought 40 days was divine, one day for Jesus's fast.

Slipping off to sleep I said my prayers. *I may not understand Your intentions, but I shall allow You to develop my life according to Your plans. I ask to be spared suffering, filled with joy, and granted safety. Thy will be done. Amen.*

I aspired not to ask for certain things to happen or tell God what He should do. I desired to allow God the time along with space to act on my behalf and trusted God knew perfectly well what was best for me.

Najera to Granon

CHAPTER 17

SEPTEMBER 17TH, 2012

I departed early as always with a planned destination of Santo Domingo de la Calzada, almost 21 kilometers (13 miles). As I began the trek, my knee felt okay. However, I decided not to take the six-kilometer detour to Canas to see the Monasterio San Millan. I am sure it would have been worth it. The description sounded amazing with its 13th century relics. But I did not want to risk my knee pain flaring up again, especially since I planned to complete one and a half stages today. Most of the paths were wide country tracks, offering remoteness and tranquility.

I arrived in Santo Domingo de la Calzada in the early afternoon. I decided not to spend the night, instead I remained just a few hours to sightsee. The city had delightful winding streets with unique architecture. I visited the Cathedral, and a museum dedicated to Mother Teresa. The construction of the Cathedral began in 1158. It was always linked to the pilgrimage of St. James. It was pastoral inside. I sensed an overpowering salvation as I strolled through. I perceived a higher power protecting me. Contained in one section, a marvelous Renaissance altarpiece. The intriguing aspect was the Gothic Henhouse which intertwined with it. A live hen and rooster lived inside it as homage to the Hen and the Rooster miracle.

The legend told of a German pilgrim, called Hugonell, who was walking to Santiago with his parents on pilgrimage when they rested at an inn in Santo Domingo de la Calzada. The owner of the inn's daughter immediately fell in love with Hugonell; sadly, her feelings were not reciprocated. The girl became angered, placed a silver cup into his luggage and accused the boy of theft. It reminded me of when Joseph did the same to a younger brother in Egypt. Thieves at that time were punished by hanging, that was the fate of Hugonell. His parents, saddened by his death, continued their pilgrimage. Upon completing the trip in Santiago de Compostela, they began their return journey to visit the grave of their dead son. When they revisited Santo Domingo, they found their son still hanging in the gallows, miraculously alive. Hugonell, excited, said to them: "Santo Domingo brought back my life. Please, go to the Mayor's house and ask him to take me down." Quickly, the parents arrived at his house and told him of the miracle. The Mayor, who was preparing to have dinner with friends, responded, "that boy is as alive as those two roasted chickens we are about to eat!" Suddenly, the chickens came to life, sprouted feathers, beaks, and crowed. And so, to this day there was a saying about the town which goes: "Santo Domingo of the Way, where roosters crow after being roasted."

After completing the sightseeing self-tour. I moved on to Granon, approximately eight more kilometers. When I reached Granon, I thought about walking even further. Ten minutes outside of town I returned. Granon was mentioned many times as a marvelous location for an evening, primarily for the Parish Albergue. A gentleman I interacted with along the path, on my return mentioned the albergue was an excellent choice for the night. I followed the advice and remained the evening.

Today, like most of my recent days, I trekked mostly alone. I sensed the desire of fellowship. The positive of the albergue, which was part of a church, offered music, mass, and a communal dinner—it sounded like what I required.

After checking in and performing my daily rituals, I entered the church. Though primitive, yet it offered a calm, comforting environment. Inside the temperature was crisp. I zipped up my wool fleece to the top and shoved my hands deep into my pockets. Between the interminable day's walk and the serene atmosphere inside I yawned, fighting the urge of dozing off. Sitting on the wooden pew, my shoulders slumped.

After sitting for about an hour observing the artwork and appreciating the peaceful atmosphere for prayer, I returned to the albergue. A wonderful spectacle inside unveiled itself, 44 pilgrims performing a task as an immense group, better yet, a family. I diced carrots, while others pre-pared onions with potatoes and set the two long, wooden tables. The tables reminded me of what I saw in the castle of Braveheart, when the nobles shared a meal together. Af-ter preparations, they sent the food off to the local bakery. During the free time I attended mass. I did not understand the language, but I loved being present and observing. I whispered my own prayers and sat and stood as everyone else did, then exited when they started communion. Not as glamorous a service as the larger churches I had attended, nevertheless, the ritual remained spiritual. I wished I knew what the priest said to the people, to follow along.

Upon completion of mass, I returned to the albergue for dinner. The hosts stated, in order to obtain our food from the local baker, we all had to parade over together. The hosts had a few of the guests dress in classic costumes of the attire from the early 1900s. Once our group arrived at the bakery, the next instructions created anxiety. The group had to sing for the baker to release our prepared meal. Bewildered and surprised by the anxiety; I have per-formed on stage as a singer, with only my guitar for sup-port. However, with a sizeable group of strangers, I became a mouse in the crowd. I attempted to hide behind other members of the group, especially when the baker asked for a song from the country you represented. Thankfully, there were a few other Americans who carried a tune as I lip sung along. After about 30 minutes of singing, the baker handed over our dinner to the four pilgrims dressed in old-world garments. We returned home and dinner served.

I was a little nervous about eating around people, sitting at the end of one table with my back to the wall. If I had to rush to the bathroom, I would have to leapfrog three other people sitting to my right. I hoped no need to vomit occurred. The meal was excellent. The first course comprised of a stew of beans with sausage, followed by baked onions, carrots along with potatoes, and dessert finished with watermelon. That meal and the "pilgrim" meals offered in all the towns were always three courses. I drank a few ounces of red wine, although it was not as good as the red wine in La Posado. Instead, I switched over to water.

Concluding dinner, each one of us stood where we were sitting at the table, introduced ourselves and told a reason for our Camino. Despite hailing from several unfamiliar countries, many of the pilgrims had remarkably similar core reasons. The common theme to strengthen a grasp of self-assurance or to observe life in a renewed perception along with having the pilgrimage accomplishment produce fresh energy. Ultimately, create insights of what to do with the rest of our lives. For the first time I believed, it surrounded me with individuals having similar thoughts as I. I was not alone or an outcast. I was content, a rarity in my life.

Amidst the completion of our stories, we all helped clean up the facility. Afterwards, the host of the albergue guided us to a special room in the church. A circular room filled with chairs attached to each other, created by hand in the 1600s. Sitting in silence, we quietly passed a wax candle around the darkened room. Holding the candle in hand with fingers intertwined, it provided a moment of reflection.

I prayed the flame from the candle ignited a wildfire inside of me to continue my soul's journey. I was transforming having faith I was embracing an authentic, higher natural realm of existence. I was attaining happiness in life's simple pleasures.

Granon to Villafranca Montes
de Oca

CHAPTER 18

SEPTEMBER 18TH, 2012

Closing the door to the albergue, I gazed over my shoulder one last time. The weathered, wooden cross over the door illuminated in the predawn light. Another day upon me with clear skies.

The walk today, mostly by the major highway. The chaotic markings of yellow arrows were a little confusing, but I knew I was okay since the highway guided me properly to Belorado, the original destination. At moments, I thought rain may appear because of an introduction of a mist. In preparation, I dressed in my rain gear, and then it stopped—of course. I saw a lot of other pilgrims had a simple cheap parka they threw over themselves, which covered their entire body as well as their backpack. The biggest issue with the parka, if there was a powerful wind you may be strangled or whipped with the material.

As the midmorning, slightly grey skies watched over me, I met a guy from South Africa of similar age, who shared his personal decisions for the Camino. He believed he was unsatisfied with the locked-into routine he was living. He desired to understand the world in a manner to allow freedom and sense a renewed purpose in his personal life. A common theme arising from the individuals I interacted with.

Throughout the day, I reconnected with previous travel companions, like Mags from Ireland. Again, those communications were brief, as pace determined the interactions. Though I welcomed the tranquility solitude allowed, it was comforting to know I was not alone out here. Countless pilgrims perceived themselves at a crossroads in their life. I, at a similar state of mind. Unfortunately, over a week into the pilgrimage, I was still hoping for some breakthrough in my thinking—or something. Was a grand idea coming like a lightning bolt? Or perhaps I would interact with someone who may change my perspectives. It was all an unknown. I walked without worry or anxiety, attempting not to place expectations or ponder the how. Simply focused on each step with my vision forward.

I arrived in Belorado, a village of about 2,100 people considered the stopping point for stage 10. I stopped in a church, built in the 16th century, titled the Church of Santa Maria. I prayed for my fellow pilgrims but also for continued strength and wellness. Afterwards, I continued towards St. Juan de Ortega.

Around 1:00 p.m. I arrived in Villafranca Montes de Oca with St. Juan de Ortega another 13 kilometers further. Due to a 1,000-meter-plus climb outside of town, I paused for the evening and rested.

Villafranca de Montes de Oca had a population of about 200 people. The positive aspect for me, they had a pharmacy to purchase some items for foot care and my achy knee. I stayed at the San Anton Abad; a recommended albergue on the forum.

The funny story of the day began with the word *Oca,* the Spanish word for goose. Outside the albergue, a flock of geese paraded around. I guess I scared one, or came across as an enemy, because it attacked me by biting at my leg causing blood to drip down my lower leg. It provided an instant memory about my mom. She owned a pet goose when she was young. She told stories of how it chased and attacked my three uncles. It created a moment of home sickness being away from family.

Although last night was a blessing in Granon, I decided on a solitary night. I guess my introverted ways required a battery charge. Sitting on my bunk, I prepared my backpack for tomorrow and headed to bed, for hopefully a restful sleep, as the sun was departing outside.

I trusted tomorrow my spirit would take me to where I needed to go. *"Guide my steps, Lord, and heal my aches and pains."*

Villafranca Montes de Oca To Burgos

CHAPTER 19

SEPTEMBER 19TH, 2012

What a lengthy day, I walked over 40 kilometers. Beginning at 5:00 a.m., I thought I would be ahead of other pilgrims and arrive to Burgos early enough to ensure a bed at an albergue of my choosing. Unfortunately, those plans changed.

Natural paths consumed most of the day. The climb from Villafranca until Ermita Valdefuente proved difficult for me, creating pain in my left foot and right ankle. Each step jolted shockwaves of misery. It forced me to stop and rest for a while. The pain diminished slightly, so I pressed onto St. Juan de Ortega. I paused again to sightsee for an hour, while snapping a few pictures, before heading on to the destination for the day, Burgos.

Outside of St. Juan toward Burgos, the landscape offered primarily flat ground through the countryside of tiny villages with a peaceful ambience. Unfortunately, I hit another painful wall around Atapuerca. I paused at the Cruz de Madre cross to ease my suffering as I saw Burgos in the distance from my viewpoint. I told myself, *even with pain—I shall reach Burgos.* I nudged and forced my aching self to continue forth with all of my dwindling supplies of energy.

The atmosphere changed instantly as I limped, almost dragging my leg, into Burgos. Entering a city of 170,000, as you can imagine—the sounds of traffic, horns, as well as with people—was the opposite to what I had enjoyed most of my day.

I arrived in Burgos with a pain scale of seven out of ten, my pace reduced to that of a snail. Two gentlemen asked if I was okay. The one gentleman, a pleasant man in his fifties. The other trekker appeared in his late sixties with unkept wild white hair and filthy feet because of wearing flip flops. Overall, both were cordial. they slowed their pace to ensure I arrived safely in Burgos.

The three of us reached the albergue around 4:00 p.m. Unluckily, the albergue and the others mentioned to us were all full. The only options were to consider a private hotel or keep walking out of town. Originally, I pondered to use Burgos as a rest day, by remaining two nights to allow proper resting and to visit their Cathedral.

Due to my faltering pace, I shared a hotel room with the two pilgrims. Part of me felt obligated to remain with them based on their generosity of time and concern. However, when the hotel stated a room for three cost 23-euros each an inner voice wanted me to disappear into the crowd.

The primitive room provided three beds along with a private bathroom. I refreshed the best I could with a shower. As I gazed into the mirror, I appeared pale or sick.

My face showcasing exposed cheekbones instead of its normal roundness. Instead of the peach colored Florida tan, I had become crème colored. Though my stomach seemed pudgy, I appeared gangly. Afterwards, I stretched out onto a bed, skipping dinner. As I laid inside my sleeping bag, I closed my eyes contemplating how my spirit was beaten down. I perceived myself at my lowest point upon the journey so far. Was its today's pain or because the albergue was full? Did my physical appearance create my perception? Or from not eating properly as I attempted to remain at my per diem? I could not grasp the words or thoughts to answer those questions. Without the ability to psychoanalyze myself, I had faith Mother Nature would smile upon me tomorrow with healing and a rejuvenated spirt.

Suddenly, I became frustrated with the older gentleman in the middle of the night. His phone created obnoxious sounds piercing through my ears, forcing an untimely awakening. He either did not understand or know how to turn it off as the room remained filled with the squawking. In addition, he was an intense snorer who wallowed on his bed. All in all, I may have gotten the worse night of sleep since being on the Camino, even worse than my first night on the kitchen mattress.

Perhaps God wanted that to happen. It may have been a lesson of patience or to sense empathy toward someone who may not see the world or others in the same way I do. The Camino de Santiago was not a private tour. I recalled interacting with over 180 people from 82 countries. The albergues infused with men, women, and sometimes children from all over the world. It required empathy to maintain sanity, as well learn valuable lessons on tolerance. I was currently failing miserably. I only desired to throw the phone out the window and stuff a pillow over his head to stop the snoring and snorting.

Burgos To Rabé de las Calzadas

CHAPTER 20

SEPTEMBER 20TH, 2012

When I awoke, instead of planning a day of sightseeing and checking into an albergue or a hotel room just for me, I allowed my poor mental state to dictate my actions. I only desired to exit out of town speedily and have alone time. With a facade of a smile, I told the gentlemen, "goodbye and Buen Camino."

When I began from the private hotel, I was surprised how far away the Cathedral de Santa Maria location was. I paused as I approached it to snap pictures. The exterior of the Cathedral was an imposing site with its architecture. Too early to enter, I did not want to wait two-hours until it opened. As I slowly trekked away, a sense of regret filled my mind knowing that was probably a once-in-a-lifetime opportunity.

On my way out of town I chose the path by the Rio Arlanzon. The soothing sounds corrected my attitude. My smile returned and the temporary cloud of despair lifted. Additionally, I was blessed with no pain.

I arrived in the city of Rabé de las Calzadas before siesta began, 2:00 p.m. to 5:00 p.m., when everything was closed. I returned to a state of irritability and tiredness because I had not eaten enough food, and I needed to sleep badly. I was becoming mentally and physically drained. *I want to finish, please let me finish my Camino.*

After checking into the albergue, I located access to WIFI in order to check plane fares back to Florida. I was appalled how much the cost to fly home on a one-way ticket. Discouraged by the price, I purchased the airplane ticket home anyway for October 18th at almost $900, I could have paid that for a round-trip ticket if I had known my travel dates before I departed. I still had to purchase transportation from Santiago to Madrid on October 17th. I attempted to block out the financials, unfortunately, the increasing demands were forcing me to decrease my daily expenditures on my pilgrimage. I began with a goal of 25-euros a day, already a miniscule amount according to other pilgrims. Now I pondered reducing it even more.

As I became comfortable in my bed, I meditated on the positive things which have happened so far. I attempted to understand my attitude change yesterday. I wounded my own soul with my thoughts of frustration, trying to discover what made me become irritable. I normally possess much more patience and understanding.

With hands clasped, I promised myself to return to my overjoyed self and to be excited by the landscapes. Every day was an adventure of images I have never seen before.

Rabé de las Calzadas to Castrojeriz

CHAPTER 21

SEPTEMBER 21ST, 2012

They shook me into wakefulness. Even under the Ambien and the earplugs, the people in the room woke me up with their snoring. Instead of continued tossing and turning, I gathered my belongings and departed at about 2:00 A.M. The goal of the day, reach Castrojeriz, about 20 kilometers (12.6 miles) away.

Departing now meant I had almost five hours before first light. With it being dark, I ambled slowly. I did my best to ensure I followed the yellow markers. When a town was listed in my guidebook, I was positive I remained on the correct path.

I paused for a momentary snack break in Hornillos del Camino by sitting on a community bench, a small quaint town, with a population of 100. The air filled with silence as everyone remained in a dream state. Before departing, I visited the Fuente del Gallo. Unfortunately, I could not see the details of the Hen Fountain with just my head torch.

The path continued through the Meseta. I felt positive surrounded by the peaceful sounds of nature and no traffic. However, with no shade I knew it could become hot as the day progressed into the afternoon with the sun rising high.

Once again, my left heel and right knee began hurting every step. Each step seemed like someone drove a sharp pin into those body parts. Like a soldier, I pressed on—fighting through the discomfort to reach the destination.

I maintained through the starless night until about 4:00 A.M. Anxiety built throughout my mind; I began sensing something wrong. I must have missed a yellow marker and began walking in the wrong direction. I no longer saw any posted along my path. The trek intersected a few crossroads. I had to choose a direction blindly. I must have gotten myself confused. Pausing in blackness, I gazed at the guidebook for answers, using my only light source, the headlamp. I only saw fields of dirt. Standing alone, I wondered whether I should stop until light or turn around and attempt to retrace my steps. Instead, I continued with building anxiety and frustration on the current path.

I scanned behind me from time to time, perhaps I would see another headlamp. It was not uncommon for other pilgrims to begin before the sun rose. Instead, two red eyes reflected the light from my head torch. An animal began following me or, worse yet, tracking me. I imagined and prayed it was an innocent fox. It commenced playing a game of hide and seek with me. It either would come up behind me, halting at about 50 yards away, or go dashing to the right of me into the fields and out of sight. A few chills of nervousness upon my spine developed. I grasped my knife as a defense, just in case, and threw rocks in its direction, trying to scare it away. As the time continued, images of Jason and Freddy arose, or even the guy from the Texas Chainsaw Massacre. I could sense my hairs standing on end on the back of my neck. I attempted to maintain reason: I am okay, only a playful fox, and not something else—like a mountain lion preparing to pounce on me for breakfast. Finally, after a couple miles, or about an hour, it left me alone. I never saw a body, only the two circular red eyes the size of marbles.

I continued into the black night of the dirt wasteland, still observing no signs showing my location or direction. I again questioned what to do, though sensed I walked too far to turn back. When I approached another crossroad without markings, I pondered to lay down and take a nap until the sun rose or another traveler awoke me. I dressed in my rain gear to ensure I covered my skin to protect myself the best I could. I had a trash bag in my backpack which I used to cover the ground. I curled up in a ball, with my backpack as the pillow, and drifted off into a nap.

As I awoke around 7:00 A.M., I spied buildings and cars in the distance. I had the sensation of being saved, like you seen in the movies of castaways seeing a ship on the horizon. I arose from my resting place, slung my belongings upon my back, and headed in their direction. The town, called Yuleada, regrettably, was far from where I should be.

A local set me on the right path, and I verified it with two others for my peace of mind. Leaving the town's boundaries, a road sign appeared for where I was going—20 kilometers away. Obviously, down cast being so far away from where I was supposed to be, I sensed all of my positive energy being swept away from my body. I took a Rocky Balboa punch to the gut. I could have easily screamed out in disbelief and madness at myself. I took pride in myself to always do the correct thing and not make mistakes. I strived for perfection. I thought about hitchhiking into town, instead of trekking the long arduous concrete. With a few breaths, I calmed myself. I placed my left foot forward and began the trek into Castrojeriz. Upon arriving at 5:00 p.m., instead of the 11:00 A.M. I should have arrived, the two albergues I wanted to stay in were full. Being denied a bed, I slumped down on a bench and removed my pack to relieve the soreness of my shoulders and create a plan of action.

The priority became food. I chose the cheapest item on the menu of a local establishment. I had no clue what I was eating. The meat—or perhaps vegetable—was red, soft, had seeds and cheese on hard bread with no condiments. I devoured as much as I could of the tasteless meal. I knew I had not been eating enough lately. I could cinch my belt one notch tighter.

Exhausted on the bench with a half-filled stomach, I pondered options for shelter. I contemplated moving on to the next city, another 10 kilometers. I proposed walking until sunset or until I collapsed with fatigue. Then I would use the trash-bag-on-the-ground technique, cover myself with my rain gear, and sleep under the stars for one night. The father figure in *The Way* experienced a similar ordeal. He became stranded in between two towns and plopped himself under a few shrub-like trees and entered dreamland.

If I attempted camping out, at least no one would snore or use their white head lamp to pack their bag in the morning and disturb everyone. Normally, the Camino de Santiago was not a camping pilgrimage. I never met any individuals using a tent or hammock. Instead of implementing the forward progression plan, I tried one other place in Castrojeriz. Through a blessing it had beds and a bottom bunk. I overflowed with joy and relief. Once again, a higher power granted what I needed.

What a day it was!

Castrojeriz To Fromista

CHAPTER 22

SEPTEMBER 22ND, 2012

At 5:05 A.M. the over-the-horizon ring tone roused me. I pressed the dismiss button. I was too drowsy to awaken. Eventually, I silently spoke to myself to begin the day. I realized, by delaying my departure, I would have to deal with more sun and heat today off of the Meseta. The barren landscape reminded me as if I were walking through Mississippi. The locals have already harvested the fields on both sides, the land only desolate dirt fields with no crops.

The 25-kilometer trek to Fromista afforded sweltering conditions. Beads of sweat trickled down my back, causing my shirt to stick to my skin. With no hat, my face charred underneath the rays of the sun. Frequently, I had to pause under the shade of a standing tree and quaff water to help my cotton mouth.

On the bright side, I visited multiple churches. I was always in awe of the relics and tapestries they possessed. The stone walls created a refreshing interior, especially compared to the outside warmth. Inside, the details of the alters were astonishing. The craftsmanship of the wood carvings beyond marvelous. One church offered wax candles and provided free matches. I scratched the red wooden head across the brown raised cardboard igniting itself into a crimson flame. The blaze danced above the white tea base. Gazing upon the ballet, I sat upon an ancient wooden pew sitting alone in silent prayer. Opening my eyes, I perceived a cleansing of negative thoughts as they saturated me in the harmonious sanctuary.

The Albergue Canal de Castilla provided shelter for the night. For some reason not many people were there. Not only did I have a bottom bunk, but several bunk beds separated me from other pilgrims.

As I curled inside the sleeping bag, I spent some time visualizing my dream life: the freedom to travel, write, compose, along with inspire and add value to the world.

I had faith I could achieve anything.

Fromista to Carrión de los Condes

CHAPTER 23

SEPTEMBER 23RD, 2012

Today began the third week of my quest for St. James. I departed around 6:00 A.M. The goal of the day reach Carrión de los Condes about 20.5 kilometers (12.7 miles) away. The quick route remained by the asphalt highway, however, I always searched to go off the beaten path. I chose a wooded path along the river. It was worth the extra distance. I walked by the Rio Ucieza for almost nine kilometers. Additionally, the path presented two churches I could visit.

Along the path less traveled, I met a pleasant German man. I learned through conversation he was 20 years old and planning to celebrate his 21st birthday in Santiago. I thought a marvelous way to mark your 21st birthday. I reminisced my 21st, 18 years ago, all I did was stop at a convenience store, bought a beer, and drank it alone. I guess my solitude had always been part of my life. Even in a crowded room, most of the time, I perceived myself alone.

The path grievously turned toward the major road once I reached the Virgen del Rio. A haze simmered above the asphalt as four-tire-concrete coffins zoomed by swiftly. I never understood why pilgrims choose the hectic boisterous highway, instead of the beautiful, serene natural pathways the Camino offered. Exiting the peace and silence of the river back into traffic was never fun for me.

Carrión de los Condes had a population of about 2,400 people. Like most of the recent towns or villages, it had a medieval atmosphere which I found refreshing. Most all of those towns contained at least one church, or usually a few. They all incorporated some monument, sculpture, or painting which blew your mind with its beauty. Upon arrival, there were many closed shops due to it being Sunday.

I settled in for the evening. My mind bounced back to before I embarked on my Camino. I had friends and family thinking I lived in a fantasy world. They asked how I could believe in such illogical things. I protected myself with an invisible bubble from their negativity and believed my personal philosophy was not senseless as I sought to courageously experience opportunities which I may never have considered or been too reluctant to pursue. I believed the majority of the world, including those personal friends and family endured within dispirited situations. They did not have the moxie to break with conformity and transform their lives.

On the other hand, I had a free spirit and a fascination with adventure. I trusted life would materialize from the confrontations of new experiences. I wanted to explore the astonishing events which God constructed. An intention of

mine was to consistently advance into new realms of experiences. I had the bravery.

I daydreamed myself into a trance, inquisitively regard-
ing what was out there.

Carrión de los Condes to Terradillo de
los Templarios

CHAPTER 24

SEPTEMBER 24TH, 2012

Today's trek demanded about eight hours. During my walk I interacted, briefly, with a pleasant woman from Holland. Like most of my encounters you speak momentarily, wish each other "Buen Camino", and one moves on from another. It was what allowed you to connect to so many people from around the world. Some pilgrims always seemed to be in a group and then others, like myself, preferred to be solo taking in the moment without interruption. It reminded me of Henry David Thoreau's quote, "I love to be alone. I never found the companion that was so companionable as solitude."

I pondered how immense my possibilities were. With my background as a certified physician assistant and past experiences as a certified athletic trainer, I had the skills for abounding opportunities around the world. However, I genuinely wanted to remain committed to my dreams, rather than return to the hamster wheel of trading time for money. The dream life I visualized, (living an artistic life filled with love, travel, experiences along with providing the world inspiration and value) created an independent freedom similar to an eagle soaring at unimaginable heights.

I reached my desired destination of Terradillos de los Templarios. It had a population of about 80, a simple village which reminded me of my hometown—population 36. They considered it the halfway point between St. Jean de Pied de Port and Santiago de Compostela.

I stayed in the Albergue Jacques de Molay. The albergue had a pleasing atmosphere. It offered no public kitchen, but the host family cooked dinner and breakfast. The country boy inside of me smiled. The home cooked meal with a gathering of fellow travelers seemed like a memorial to Sunday dinners at Granny Ray's house with the family. As we settled into our wooden chairs, the ceramic bowls passed around the table clockwise. Even though the dinner was saturated with conversations, I settled into a quiet mood. Since Burgos I have not been in a talkative frame of mind. I bypassed opportunities to sit around with others and drink at night. Instead, I desired only the provided bunk and security of my sleeping bag.

I stretched out supine then curled into the fetal position. I realized I had to locate my internal joy and had to do it by myself.

Terradillos de los Templarios To
Calzadilla de los

SEPTEMBER 25TH, 2012

When I departed the albergue, the heavens looked like they were opening up with apricot hues. The planned destination was Calzadilla de los, nearly 25–30 kilometers (16 miles). Most of the track ran parallel to the N-120 highway until I located a path less traveled near Caza de Coto. The fresh trail offered peace along with remoteness with only sounds produced besides my rubber soles were the local sheep in the nearby pastures.

The morning manifested bitterly cold. Goosebumps erupted from my arms until the application of a warm fleece pullover dulled them. Today's wind blew me around. When I glanced back, my steps staggered in the dust, instead of a straight line.

I listened to Genesis today while walking on the Bible app. I almost cried twice listening to it. Genesis means birth. It related how the Universe was created. I believed between the soothing voice, powerful words, and surrounding landscape; a revitalized sense of alertness began. I was becoming new, seeing life in a renewed light. I trusted continued prayer along the Camino would produce a strengthened faith. The enthusiasm of my pilgrimage set the stage for the next chapter of my life.

I reached Calzadilla de los. I stayed in a donation albergue, those albergues are lovely, and serve their purpose, but never had hot water. The sleeping quarters were small, and the public area was only a few feet away from my bed.

As the skies transitioned into evening, it began raining. I sat by a four-paned window watching the rain fall. The outside dirt path transitioned into a murky stream. I remained in silence, listening to the orchestra the drops of rain on the roof produced. A flash of thought buzzed through my mind, *was all the effort utterly worth it?* After a few moments of muteness, I decided it was. Life was fleeting and should be filled with experiences. What an adventure the Camino de Santiago was. I told myself to continue gaining experiences in my life, no matter what obstacles may arise.

Calzadilla de los To Villarente

CHAPTER 26

SEPTEMBER 26ᵀᴴ, 2012

I awoke before dawn's early light. I dressed in my convertible hiking pants, t-shirt, wool jacket, and my Toggs rain jacket for extra warmth, slipping on a headband, to ensure my ears remained toasty, along with gloves. After lacing my hiking shoes, I descended the stairs silently into the open air.

I maintained enthusiasm today. I was pleased for what I had accomplished up to that point. My sense of accomplishment extended beyond my personal pilgrimage to my life experiences. Memories of working TV commercials as an actor, working on the medical staff of the Miami Dolphins, and the time I spent providing coverage for the 2002 Winter Olympics in Salt Lake City started building a sense of confidence in me. I thought, *I can conquer the world.*

The left-right cadence progressed until I reached Mansilla de las Mulas at noon. Mansilla had a population of about 1,000 people, considered a province of Leon. The town had a unique medieval wall built in the 12ᵗʰ century which welcomed a pilgrim to the city.

After some personal debate, I kept walking further, another six kilometers to Villarente, which was, unfortunately, by a major highway. I was not alone in my decision; many other pilgrims making those extra steps.

The albergue resembled a mountain lodge with a wood stove to the right of the main door providing warmth along with the aroma of burnt oak. The open public area offered plenty of sofas and chairs to lounge around on. Not to mention, a plethora of open beds which meant I snagged a bottom bunk. To create privacy for my bunk, I attached a bungee cord from one end of the bed to the other and then used clothespins to create a curtain with my bath towel.

While relaxing on a sofa, a young Spanish man offered me a bag of chips as he passed by. I hoped it was not because he could hear my stomach growling. After devouring the snack, I strolled to the local market. I returned with angel-hair pasta and a jar of sauce. While preparing my meal in the communal kitchen, a fellow pilgrim gave me additional noodles. The added noodles included fresh vegetables, which made my dinner much more nutritious. Through the Pilgrim's generosity, I ate until my stomach ballooned outwards almost forcing me to undo my top button for expansion. The fullness sensation was rare for me because of my limited budget. I ate my meal in their company. Those minor acts of kindness and generosity took place every day on the Camino.

After dinner, I returned to a hidden sofa to relax my filled belly. Lying supine, thoughts of my future, post Camino, arose. I weighed the pros and cons of either: a teaching position, in my birth state of Mississippi, or returning to active practice in orthopedic surgery. I knew I could always return to physical practice; I would not forget how that was done. Perhaps the teaching position would be the only time I had that opportunity. An opportunity, not only to teach, but to return to Mississippi and be near family that had grown distant.

Villarente To Leon

CHAPTER 27

SEPTEMBER 27TH, 2012

Approaching Leon, with a population of over 130,000, I prepared myself for the city life again. I kept a wary eye on traffic as I did not want the hood of a car to end my Camino. The monastery I desired to stay at was closed upon arrival, cleaning up from the night before. I sat around out front with a few other early arrivals. I remained nearby to ensure I got a bed and, hopefully, a bed of my choice.

Upon the opening, I checked into the monastery, Albergue Santa Maria de Carbajal, a Benedictine monastery. The nuns created a wonderful, calming atmosphere. The one rule, a strict 9:30 p.m. curfew. After curfew, a pilgrim's benediction was offered in the chapel, then lights out at 10:30 p.m. Many fellow pilgrims stayed in a hotel for more freedom and, perhaps, stay an extra day for rest. Besides, a hot shower and private bathroom would be a welcomed, well-deserved luxury.

Leon's charm captured me. Although a large city, it emerged not as congested. I sensed freedom of space as I walked or rested in the plazas, especially the Plaza Mayor. The Plaza seemed the key hub for people watching and consumed with shops, bars, as well as restaurants. I saw amazing structures like the 17th century Baroque Town Hall. Leon offered a maze of streets branching off the plaza to other interesting treasures. I traversed around for hours snapping pictures, gazing upon statues and the architecture.

I rediscovered Michael from Germany during my wanderings. We visited the Cathedral de Santa Maria de Leon. I paid the extra euros for the self-guided tour, a set of recordings explaining the different statutes and features of the cathedral. It was beyond amazing. The time it must have taken to carve the detailed woodwork was difficult to fathom.

It may have been the city of Leon or an inner desire, but I surmised I needed to spend some time with other people for fellowship. I thought back to Granon and a warm sensation entered my chest. Within minutes of those thoughts, an invitation out to dinner with seven other people occurred. One pilgrim introduced had compiled over 2,000 miles. He was flying home later that night. I sampled tapas for the first time. Tapas were similar to an appetizer and had a price of under 5-euro. The dish of potatoes was tasty. We all shared some deviled eggs which were wondrous as well.

We all sat at a long table, wrapping around to continue our conversations. I ordered lasagna for my entrée, while most of the group ordered spaghetti. It worried me I had made the wrong choice when it took 15 minutes longer for my food to arrive. When my lasagna arrived, I laughed out loud—it had a serving size of about five bites compared to the overflowing spaghetti dishes. Unfortunately, another member of our group had it even worse than I did. He ordered the fish specialty which never arrived. When the waiter was politely asked when the meal would be served, with a down cast frown, he stated he forgot to put the order in with the chef. With sincere apology, he swiftly paced to the kitchen. However, when the clock struck 9:00 p.m., only 30 minutes to the monastery curfew, the order had not been delivered. The individuals who ordered the massive spaghetti dinners offered to share their leftovers, though he declined. The restaurant apologized and offered a fresh meal, but there was not much which could be done—we raced back through the streets of Leon to beat the curfew.

The monastery doors locked behind us. Then, the nuns guided anyone interested in a prayer into a small chapel. The quaint room filled with wooden pews and spiritual pictures offered a wonderful experience. It reminded me of the genuine nature of my journey—time to reflect. I thought about miracles. The Bible told of miracles performed by Jesus throughout the New Testament. The person only needed to maintain unwavering faith. Even in the media I saw stories of miracles relayed, they always ended with people thanking God. Confidently, I expected they would happen in my life. I was sure my life was changing.

Leon to Villas de Mazarife

CHAPTER 28

SEPTEMBER 28TH, 2012

When I awoke, I considered purchasing a hotel room to stay another night in Leon. I wanted to splurge on rest, enjoy a private room and bathroom, and have the opportunity for a late evening of fun. The elegant hotel from the movie *The Way* promoted a pilgrim's special of $100 a night. Instead, I exited the city. I had to allow finances to dictate my decision.

Upon leaving, I examined the Camino markings. Each one was a raised, discreet shell, resembling a golden artifact attached to the street. The Camino shell offered another fine detail to stow away in my memory.

About two kilometers outside of Leon, I crossed a spectacular 16th century stone bridge which crossed the River Bernesga. It offered a gateway from city life to the return of country life. The landscapes no longer filled with towering buildings or bustling streets of people. Now, all I could see were the Castilian cereal fields.

When I arrived in Villar de Mazarife, there was no-where to bunk for the evening. Discouraged, I reviewed the guidebook. The next official location was another 14–15 kilometers away. Gazing over-the-horizon, I lost confidence in myself to endure the distance. I expanded my chest fully for a deep breath. Though already fatigued, I moved forward with no choice. Luckily, I came across a new albergue, which opened only a month ago. I was thankful as I hit the proverbial wall. Inside the albergue were hard-wood floors, marble stairs, porcelain knobs, and brand-new beds. However, the true blessing, only three pilgrims checked in. It may not have been totally private, but close. It provided another instance where I saw God and the Camino guiding my decisions. Not only did I have an almost private room, it saved me $94. The three of us spread out in the room, to give each other privacy and allow plenty of solitude. An added benefit, the owners prepared dinner for us, an intimate gathering of five. Though I remained my normal, quiet self, preferring to listen rather than speak. It allowed the exact amount of socializing I required without crossing the invisible line of irritation or desire to sprint into isolation. It produced a toothy grin, laughter, and a sensation of joy inside my heart. The albergue was a true blessing.

Villas de Mazarife to Astorga

CHAPTER 29

SEPTEMBER 29TH, 2012

Today marked the end of twenty-one days along my personal pilgrimage. Today's journey ended in Astorga, almost 30-kilometers (19-plus miles).

I departed before the sun. As I watched the sunrise over the landscape, it created an idyllic scene, washed in a peaceful ambience. The trek was relatively solitary along natural paths, which I adored greatly. A unique structure located before Hospital de Órbigo; a 13th century medieval bridge. They considered it one of the longest in Spain. As I crossed, my imagination rolled with imagines of knights on horses entering the town.

Fatigue overwhelmed me today. I directed my throbbing legs and feet, which seemed like petrified stumps, into Astorga. I checked into the Albergue St. Javier in proximity to their cathedral.

After checking in and performing a few daily duties, I hit the streets for about an hour. I decided, instead of the albergue kitchen, to grab lunch locally, pondering tapas.

When I came on my pilgrimage, I told myself I did not want to eat the normal American diet, especially fast food. I desired to try local dishes from the different regions. Sticking to my guns, I entered a restaurant to try its local cuisine. I ordered a local soup dish. However, what exited the kitchen was a gigantic bowl of broth with things floating in it. Some meat had skin still on it. I tried to eat most of it as I was hungry. But the flavors were not for my taste buds, a waste of eight euros. After the lunch experiment, I ran into a pilgrim who I met earlier that day. He was a chef, using the Camino to experience the food and add to his menu upon his return, so I asked him what I ate. He stated it contained pig ear, pig tongue, chicken, lamb, and beef. Luckily, I did not know the ingredients until after I sampled it. Another memory for the books.

Astorga offered a plethora of options for the adventurer at heart, similar to Leon only smaller. The Cathedral St. Marta, which included a museum, was amazing. Built in the 15th century with a gothic appeal. As all cathedrals the artwork, carvings, and sculptures were beyond inspirational. As I walked around, I marveled at the detail. I sensed peace and joy through those cities and countryside. I could be alone without feeling lonely.

Though the albergue contained a community kitchen, I splurged for a Pilgrim's meal for my dinner. Besides, lunch was not too filling. I strolled through the streets gazing over different menus, considering which one I would fancy the most. I chose a little restaurant around the corner from the albergue. Sitting alone, an older grey-haired gentleman, fashionably dressed in a jacket, asked to share my table. Upon introductions, I learned he was from Hungary. The meal's first course, a fresh beef stew, followed by a roasted chicken leg, and completed with a tasty vanilla ice cream. The shared conversation was pleasant. We discussed our experiences so far along the Camino. Secretly, I told myself I should do that more often instead of always being alone. The basis of the Camino de Santiago was brotherhood and community, a family.

Astroga to Foncebadon

CHAPTER 30

SEPTEMBER 30TH, 2012

I departed with a descending full moon above, as I trekked along a goat tracked road. I walked continuously for five hours, upon undulating terrain. Pausing for a physical break, I consumed a slice of a Spanish omelet filled with eggs and potatoes. It has become my go to meal because of its tantalizing taste and affordable nature. I wished I had known about the tasty dish much sooner. Learning about what was affordable along the road was one thing I continued to chuckle about. The cost of a small glass of orange juice or a miniature aluminum canned Coke was the same as an entire bottle of local red wine.

As I strolled through the day, glaring vacantly into the distance, I saw myself as heroic. I sensed no fear of the unknown. I used my personal decisions as my guide and reason. Trusting my inner voice, which I regarded as the voice of God, I believed I could achieve anything. I no longer cared what others thought or suggested. I may listen to their input, yet, it was up to me to choose my path. Maintaining that unwavering faith, I knew God would continue to provide me for my needs.

I arrived in town while the sun still high upon the clear blue skies and the heat of the day at its highest. Foncebadon, at an elevation of 1,400 meters had a population of about 50 people. The views of the distant mountains were spectacular. The horizon appeared hundreds of miles away.

As I approached the albergue, a few new friends greeted me. Upon a decrepit stone wall of four to six feet above the dusty, tan dirt path four goats said hello by shaking their necks and allowing their bells to ring. It honored me for the admission to Foncebadon.

I checked into the Albergue Domus Dei. An 18-bed donation hostel with a shared dinner hosted by an American from San Francisco, who volunteered his time for a few weeks. I was one of the first to arrive, so I grabbed a bottom bunk. Next to the room of beds, a wooden sliding door acted as a wall. As it opened from left to right, a small chapel came into view. The small room strangely long to accommodate six-miniature pews for worship along with meditation.

As the sun settled, a group of 18 pilgrims came together for our shared dinner. It may not have been a five-star meal, but lovely in its own right. Similar to my stay in Granon, we all helped prepare vegetables, set the table, and other menial tasks. We interacted like family at a Sunday's dinner. As we passed bowls around, the conversation filled the room. Moments like those were uplifting to the soul.

After dinner, I slipped away to my bunk for a nap. An hour passed until new occupants startled me. Upon arousal, I returned into the small hamlet for a drink. Stepping outside, I hurriedly zipped my fleece jacket to the top and placed my hands under my arms to shake off the chill. I dashed to decrease the exposure to the night air. I entered the medieval-themed local bar. Sitting alone, I splurged on two beers.

Tomorrow was a special, and an anticipated day as I would arrive at the La Cruz de Ferro. It was the first place along the Camino to place a rock at its base and say a special prayer.

Foncebadon to Ponferrada

CHAPTER 31

OCTOBER 01ST, 2012

I awoke to the first day of October. Departing Fonce-badon, my steps seemed lighter as I floated with excitement. After a scant distance, La Cruz de Ferro appeared. Not only the last major scene of *The Way* I would encounter, but it also marked a ceremony of reflection. With the skies illuminated with blues, yellows, and transitioning clouds, I leaned my golden colored trekking poles against the cross. Removing my backpack, I extracted the smoothed rock, obtained in Zama, Mississippi, from the driveway of my childhood home. I clasped the rock in my hand as bountiful memories of those red, dusty dirt roads returned.

Positioned in silence, as the sun crested the horizon, I began the prayer from the movie, *The Way*,

"Lord may this stone, a symbol of my efforts on the pilgrimage that I lay at the foot of the cross, weigh the

balance in favor of my good deeds some day when the deeds of my life are judged. let it be so."

After a speechless moment, I gratefully placed the rock at its base, among the hundreds of thousands of others from over the centuries. I selfishly wanted to remain in that spot for hours, reflecting. However, hundreds of others would pass-by today, performing similar personal ceremonies. Though I still had countless miles until the ocean, it was an amazing accomplishment to reach the monument.

After the personal moment expired, I began again with a persistent and willing attitude. I had reached a purified, heightened, and organic state of existence.

I strolled in a daze observing the stagnant windmills along natural paths flung out through the mountains. Then, I reached the peak of the Camino, 1,515 meters. It offered spectacular views of the mountain top in the distance. The relaxing melody of the Arroyo de Prado stream soothed my ears.

Standing in solitude, I decreed not to fixate on my destination. As I was getting closer, I craved to embrace gratitude. The pilgrimage was what counted.

PONFERRADA

Ponferrada had a population of 62,000 people. Similar, to the larger cities of the Camino, it offered plentiful of churches, monuments, statues, and even a castle for sightseeing. The city highly regarded for its Bierzo wines. I had acquired the taste of red wine along the journey, primarily because of repetition.

I stayed at the Albergue S. Nicolas de Flue as I entered town. A donation based albergue. The albergue on the outskirts of town about two-to-three kilometers from the principal city or even a food store. That meant a lot of backtracking, which I normally attempted to avoid.

After completing a shivering shower, laundry by hand, and setting up my top bunk, I journeyed into Ponferrada. The first order of business was to get lunch. I located a local market to save euros. However, when I entered town temptation came knocking. I spotted a McDonald's sign. *I may have to break down for a big mac,* I thought. Luckily, it was about three-to-four kilometers in a different direction. Instead, I purchased turkey lunch meat, cheese slices, and bread from the local grocery store. Afterwards, I sat on a bench in the public plaza, eating as I watched people pass-by.

Ponferrada contained the Castillo de los Templarios. I was excited to see the inside of an ancient castle, but it was closed—of all days. Instead, I spent the remainder of the pleasant afternoon visiting other churches and sights, including the Basilica de la Encina and the Torre del Reloj.

I headed back to the albergue to relax. My roommate, a fleshy, older gentleman with a full greying beard and receding hairline, mentioned he was a deafening snorer. I did not think much of it as I had Ambien, ear plugs, and plenty of experience with snorers. However, well before the rooster crowed, the gentleman began his concert. I think he could have won an award for being the loudest snorer in the world. I had to exit the room at 2:00 A.M. and relocated all my belongings to the commons area, finding refuge on a sofa, escaping into a dreamless stupor.

Ponferrada to Villafranca

CHAPTER 32

OCTOBER 2ND, 2012

When I awoke, I departed instead of returning to the orchestra of snores. The hands of my watched displayed 6:30 A.M. The planned destination for the day, Villafranca del Bierzo, a 26-kilometer (15-plus mile) journey, unfortunately, mostly parallel to the intrusive highway. On the bright side, the stage afforded primarily flat terrain.

On the way out of town, I ambled past the Castillo de los Templarios castle. I really wanted to see inside. However, I knew the best course was to move on instead of staying another night for a single attraction.

Later in the morning, I crossed the Pons Ferrada, or Iron Bridge. The bridge crossed the Rio Sil. I paused. The sounds of the powerful river provided inner strength. I cherished the moment.

Today awarded a blessed day of gifts. I stopped at all the open churches on my way. I liked wandering inside, observing the artwork or sculptures, as well as sitting in the pews to say a prayer. The first church along the path offered a gift: a waterproof bag the size of a white envelope containing an email address. *How considerate,* I thought when *I have internet access, I would send a thank you.* After a few kilometers, I opened it up. "*WHOA!*" I said. The bag was not a gift; it was another pilgrim's documents which he accidentally left behind. It contained his passport, Camino credentials, money, and other important documents. After looking at his picture, I thought I spent last night in the same albergue. *That meant I may see him again tonight.* I now sensed I was on a mission to return those documents. Each time I encountered a pilgrim, I showed the gentleman's picture to ask if they knew or had seen him.

In the second church I visited, an elderly lady with bent back, gave me another gift: a piece of candy. Small tokens like those were a true blessing. I was grateful of her kindness. As I passed through Columbrianos, a modest chapel containing an alluring mural depicting a pilgrim walking along the Camino. I became lost into the image, pondering the millions of pilgrims which have trekked through those same grounds.

Noted on the forums were advice not to carry a camera. Instead, soak up everything in the present moment. Allow your mind to take you back to those places when you reminisced. I disagreed with the advice. I snapped photos of everything I could, including the delightful mural. I wanted to walk back through my Camino on a picture journey at any time. Some say a picture speaks a thousand words.

When I arrived at Villafranca, I checked into the Albergue Municipal. The town of Villafranca a marvelous city, housed seven churches, including the 12th century Romanesque Church of Santiago. It featured the Door of Forgiveness, where pilgrims unable to continue onto Santiago could receive absolution, just as they would in Santiago. Sadly, the young Italian man was not located during my travels today.

As the stars illuminated the darkened sky, I wrapped my fatigued body into my sleeping bag. I held the Italian documents asking God tomorrow to be the day I returned his valuables. I am sure he must be worried and upset. I returned them securely to my backpack then drifted off to a deep sleep.

Villafranca to La Faba

CHAPTER 33

OCTOBER 3ʳᵈ, 2012

I awoke excited. Not only has the mileage to Santiago decreased to less than 200 km, I was entering the region of Galicia, known for the rainy weather and greener landscapes. Plus, I was trekking the Dragonte detour today. I read only 5–10% of the pilgrims chose the route because of its difficulty. Though told, it would reward me with amazing views. Overall, today equaled about 35 kilometers (20-plus miles) with climbs over 1000 meters, just to descend 500 meters and then go back up to 1,300 meters.

I departed in darkness from the Albergue, once again. As the sun broke free of its prison, it illuminated the horizon with its yellow aura. Standing above the city overlooking a distant mountain dressed in clouds, I turned to continue on my way. A sensation of elation overwhelmed me as I located the first wooden sign of the Dragonte trail.

The route undulated through the Valcarce Valley. It offered rewarding mountain scenery, parts of the trail were only wide enough for one person, and the trek crossed a plethora of streams. I continuously marveled at the scenery throughout the day. I spoke with locals and shared the path with the livestock. The interactions made me feel as if I was an apostle carrying the Word. I was a pilgrim and a country boy.

In San Fiz do Seo, along the Dragonte trail, the cantina was closed. A local man, probably in his late 70s, with rough tanned skin, named Celic asked if I needed any water or food. I said, "*Thank you, but I had plenty in my backpack.*" The kind gesture provided me with comfort. I was a stranger in the land, yet, God met my needs. I glowed with an aura of gratefulness. A simple interaction like that, if it could catch like wildfire across the world, would ease suffering for many.

I wished every day were like today. The thrill of exploring, self-reflection, and adventure. I listened to the wind and sensed the dirt path beneath my feet. The silence of nature recharged an inner being I thought I lost.

Not long after Celic checked on me, I paused for my homemade lunch. I sat on a brick wall which created a water pond for animals. It stood about four feet from the ground, built from old stones and bricks. My feet dangled from the seated position. It was slightly off the main asphalt path and near the edge of a little village. I heard distant taps on the ground approaching along with a melody of bells ringing. A local farmer came into view as he guided his steers for an afternoon drink. I sat inches away from their slurping tongues and hooked, pointed horn tips. At first, I felt anxiety build through my stomach, so I moved away. The farmer assured me I was free from harm. My mood switched to awe and thankfulness as I became part of their world.

Today's scenery offered everything I expected. I have never visited Ireland or Scotland, but that place could have been their twin brother or sister. Every picture I snapped saturated with green landscapes and distant mountains.

Finally, the Dragonte detour returned to the original pilgrim's path in Herrerias. Personally, the detour was worth every grueling kilometer. I definitely considered it the road less traveled. I met only five or six other pilgrims, Celic, and a handful of two-thousand-pound steers. I perceived the presence of God surrounding me.

I entered La Faba and stayed at the Albergue Parish, highly recommended on the Camino forums as a stopping point. After such a demanding journey, my legs were like dead tree trunks. Thankfully, the albergue offered plenty of hot water. I took a well-deserved long shower. The water beads cleansed the grime away. Afterwards, two gentlemen from Germany and an American couple I had met before were preparing dinner and invited me to join them. A perfect feast of pasta, sauce, fresh vegetables, bread, and, of course, red wine. We sat around and drank three bottles of red wine while talking and laughing. A true Camino-de-Santiago evening filled with pilgrims sharing their generosity of spirit toward each other. I was profoundly indebted.

After dinner, I briefly stepped outside. The temperature was dropping rapidly. I shivered as the sky embellished from the red-orange light of the setting sun. I remained tranquil, deeply lifted, and absent in thought.

Before preparing for a night of rest, I struck up a brief conversation with the albergues host. I talked about how normally I started my days before dawn. He insisted, "wait until at least dawn, the Galician landscapes should not be missed."

Finally, surrounding myself with my sleeping bag. I thought for a moment:

I was a slave to my dream, yet thankful. I was free to act to obtain them. I was creating a second chance where I could truly follow my heart and begin a new adventurous path.

La Faba to Triacastela

CHAPTER 34

OCTOBER 4TH, 2012

I slept until 7:00 A.M. and departed about 8:30 A.M. I gazed at the sun over the mountain range. The skies were clear with minimal clouds to obstruct the fabulous views. The entire distant landscape saturated with deep dark greens. A reminder of the beauty surrounding the region of Galicia.

I walked along the path in silence until I arrived in O'Cebreiro. I visited the O'Cebreiro Iglesias to view the relics and what interesting things it may possess. The modest church constructed in the ninth century offered an internal sanctuary exhibited by a dimly lit atmosphere. Its concrete walls provided a coolness compared to the outdoor warmth. The church provided an intimate presence as I silently observed its treasures. Of all the items, an amazing poem, the *Pilgrim's Prayer,* stayed with me.

Pilgrim's Prayer
By
Fraydino

Although I may have traveled all the roads, crossed mountains, and valleys from East to West, if I have not discovered the freedom to be myself, I have arrived nowhere.

Although I may have shared all of my possessions with people of other languages and cultures; made friends with pilgrims' of 1000 paths, or shared albergue with Saints and princes, if I am not capable having my neighbor tomorrow, I have arrived nowhere.

Although I may have carried my pack from beginning to end and waited for every Pilgrim in need of encouragement or given my bed to one who arrived later than I, given my bottle of water in exchange for nothing; if upon returning to my home and work, I am not able to create brotherhood or to make happiness, peace, and unity, I have arrived nowhere.

Although I may have food and water each day and enjoyed a roof and shower every night; or may have had my injuries well attended, if I have not discovered in all that the love of God, I have arrived nowhere.

Although I may have seen all the monuments and contemplated the best sunsets; although I may have learned a greeting in every language or tasted the clean water from every fountain if I have not discovered who is the author

*so much free beauty and so much peace, I have arrived no-
where.*

*If from today I do not continue walking on your path,
searching and living according to what I have learned; in
from today I do not see in every person, friend, or foe a
companion on the Camino; if from today I cannot recog-
nize God, the God of Jesus of Nazareth as the one God of
my life, I have arrived nowhere.*

Upon completion, tears trickled down my gracious face
as my heart filled with joy. The spirit of freedom saturated
my soul. The pilgrimage along the Camino was not just a
vacation. It was meant it to be ingrained into your being
and create a spirit inside of you, no matter where you may
return in the world. I can live life as a pilgrim and display
love and generosity to all.

Departing the church, I continued on the natural paths
with small, intimate fields as well as pastures of sheep grazing. At one point, at an elevation of 1,200 meters, revealed
incredible views of Os Ancares and the O Courel Mountain
Pass. As the day progressed, I was feeling challenged with
every step. *I must still be tired from the Dragonte detour,* I
thought. I terminated my day in Triacastela.

Instead of cooking or eating a sandwich for dinner, I
had the pilgrim's meal at a local restaurant. The 10-euros
meal as always offered three wonderful courses, which included a tasty bottle of local red wine. My impoverished
body devoured the food as a ravaged wild animal with table
manners.

Sitting alone at the four-chair table, a woman behind me, probably in her 60s by the look of her graying hair, tapped me on the shoulder. She overheard my southern accent when speaking to the waiter and asked where I was from. I replied Florida but originally from Mississippi. She was from Canada, her husband from Ireland. They were sharing dinner with a couple from Israel. She asked if I was on a pilgrimage. I replied with a nod of my chin and a *"yes, ma'am."* Like most, she asked my reasons for the Camino. We began talking about my desire for a fresh way of life, instead of the hamster wheel, and the hope for insights into the next chapter of my life. I mentioned it was rare for me to enjoy a Pilgrim's Meal due to my budget of 15–20 euros per day. She asked how I was holding up on such a low budget. I explained how I managed by making a lot of my own food and not buying souvenirs along the way. She secretly took a bill from her purse and placed it in my hand. I clasped my fingers around it. At first, I did not want to open it in front of her, but she insisted. When I opened my fingers, a 50-euro bill presented. I immediately cried from her generosity. I embraced her with a hug, said thank you, and snapped a few pictures with her and her husband. Her generosity was overpowering.

When I finished my dinner, the waiter allowed me to take the remaining wine home with me. I returned to the albergue and told my friends Joe and Celina about the generosity. I began crying again. They hugged me to provide support. I let them have the remaining red wine. The couple invited me to share a glass with them, except I found myself becoming more internal—seeking solitude.

When the sun had set, the first stars made their appearance. I cuddled into my sleeping bag pondering the fact I have made many mistakes along my path in life. I believed I was getting a deeper learning of myself upon my pilgrimage. I trusted as I continued my journey with faith in God, I would arrive wherever I needed to arrive. Each day has created a desire to keep looking for meaning. I trust I shall find it.

Triacastela to Sarria

CHAPTER 35

OCTOBER 5TH, 2012

Sarria was the destination today about 25 kilometers (15.5 miles) away. Sarria, a quaint town of 13,000 people, acted as a major starting point for new pilgrims. The 100-kilometer distance to Santiago allowed a person to qualify for the Compostela, similarly to someone, like myself, walking the entire route. Originally, I was to start there myself when I had only a 10-day vacation from work. With the influx of new pilgrims, I expected a rush to find an albergue and a bed each night.

That morning towards the Benedictine Monastery of Samos, I was feeling happier. Perhaps from the unfamiliar landscapes, or still on a high from last night's interaction at dinner. When I arrived in Samos, the town wrapped itself around the monastery. One reason I was excited to visit the monastery, it was where the liquor came from in the movie *The Way*. There was even a fabled story. The Monks who brewed the liquor were blind to protect the secret formula.

I entered the 17-century monastery thinking I could walk around at my own leisurely pace. However, it was tour based. I just missed a departing tour, but the ticket master told me where they were and allowed me to go find them on my own. I crossed paths with a monk and asked if I could snap his picture, but he declined. The monastery was alluring. They decorated the walls with mural paintings, had sculptures in the outdoor gardens, and beautiful artifacts throughout. I caught up with the tour in the chapel where I sat in pews built in the early centuries.

Upon returning from the tour, I purchased the famous liquor. It would be a keepsake I would regret not purchasing. Two scenarios popped into my mind. Either open the bottle upon my retirement from a future job someday or have it drunk as a celebration at my funeral one day.

The rest of the day's pathway remained secluded, mostly wooded, almost the entire way to Sarria. I paused briefly at times to watch the lambs grazing in their fenced land.

The Sarria albergue was charming. As expected, it was full, along with an increase in price. Most albergues besides the donation ones, cost 10-euros. Tonight's lodging cost 15-euros. I knew that would probably be the story for the remainder of the way to Santiago. I even viewed charter buses with school-aged children, among others, who would make the walk from here to Santiago. Of course, their experience differed vastly from mine. They had their charter bus or vans carrying their luggage, they would walk a few hours, eat a prepared lunch, and then ride to the next city. I stopped myself from the judgment which started flowing through my mind and reminded myself: *It could be easy to look down upon those individuals, as you have walked so far carrying a heavy backpack. You must remember those recent arrivals were nervous and was the only way they could complete the Camino, because of time and schedule or health. Remind yourself to be a loving pilgrim, welcome them, offer advice and support.* I paused knowing at one time I would have been one of those people.

Lying on my bunk, my feet like wooden blocks, the surrounding people rustled through packs or tossed and turned, I grinned in patience, knowing I had a private hotel in Santiago waiting for me. I used the WIFI to check my checking account. The balance displayed $0. I transferred $2000 from my credit card into my checking account to cover possible spending.

I closed my eyes to pray. *Dear Lord, bless me with a delightful day tomorrow. I continued to ask for limited pain throughout my body. Help me maintain an open heart filled with joy. May tomorrow be the day I locate the young man with the lost belongings and ease his worry. Amen.*

I had faith my persistence would soon be rewarded.

Sarria to Portomarin

CHAPTER 36

OCTOBER 6TH, 2012

A sleepless night in the albergue. I awoke almost two-hours before dawn. Instead of returning to a restful state, I exited as I have done so many times upon the journey. As I departed, the sky barren of stars. It was Saturday, the goal, reach Portomarin, about 22 kilometers (13-plus miles).

Near sunrise, I entered an outdoor cemetery to observe the dates on the tombs. After a circular patrol, I returned to the Camino-de-Santiago trail. After another few hours, I paused at an outdoor café where over a dozen pilgrims sat soaking up the sun and enjoying a meal or snacks. I searched over their faces for the young Italian, unfortunately, nowhere to be found. I snapped a few pictures of the resting pilgrims, including a gentleman from Japan who in his early 70s.

Most of the day I tramped on a wooded track through Lilliputian style villages. I visited churches, like the Iglesia de Santiago, in Barbadello. Inside the church, a divine tympanum over the entrance door along with a statue of St. James. The weather remained pleasant for most of the time. An occasional mist occurred but being in Galicia I expected heavy rains at any time.

I walked with my thoughts today, instead of listening to the bible. I wanted my attention on the present moment. The sounds of the pebbles being stepped on, the aluminum ping of each trekking stick, along with the comforting noises of the local sheep or birds. It all enabled me to deepen my inner conversation. I began thinking about the teaching position offered before leaving for the Camino. My previous PA school program director, who had recently relocated to Mississippi asked if I had interest. The faculty position came with the same salary I was earning in Florida with the added bonus of living near relatives on my dad's side. Some of whom I have not seen in a few years. I asked God if that were where He wanted me to go, trusting a sign would appear in the remainder of my days on the quest for St. James. I told myself I could always perform a job search when I returned home as well. There are many places in the USA which would interest me to live in. Besides, I had an inner dream of writing a book about my pilgrimage, catch up on my music aspirations, and keep up my current side hustle of playing Texas Hold'em. No matter the outcome, I wanted to accomplish vast goals and observe infinite wonders.

I reached Portomarin. The quaint town, with a few cobblestoned streets, also possessed a popular main square, Praza Conde de Fenosa. Anytime I viewed a cobblestoned path my mind instantly created an image out of a Charles

Dickens's tale. The local church, San Nicolas XIIth C, opened at 8:30 p.m. for mass. After checking into the albergue, and being blessed with a bottom bunk, I showered, washed my clothes, and rested and relaxed during the siesta, 2 p.m.–5 p.m.

Alone in the room, I had the door cracked for future pilgrims to enter and some privacy. I heard a knock upon the wooden door. When I looked up, I saw a young Italian man. He was the one who I was searching for! A true blessing! It had been four days since the priest gave me the package which the youthful man accidentally left in a small church. He must have heard of me through other pilgrims as I searched for him. I returned his belongings, and he embraced me tightly with a gracious hug. He asked to take me to dinner and drinks tonight as a thank you. I declined, as I was just thankful to return his belongings, however, he insisted. I finally agreed, and we made plans to meet with his friends around 7:30 p.m. With a final hug, he departed. It saturated me with joy. I succeeded in my quest.

The siesta period expired; I exited my bunk to walk around. I ran into my friend Michael, from Germany. We shared a brief conversation how things were and promised to reconnect again soon.

As the designated time for dinner approached, excitement built. I arrived at the restaurant. Entering the open-floor plan, they set a long table for what appeared to be a dozen people. I located an empty chair amongst the group. Observing their interactions, it reminded me of a large southern lunch after church. Even though I spoke no Italian and their English was minimal, they easily communicated their loving bonds. He had a cousin who spoke moderate English, she translated, allowing me to join in on the conversations and jokes. Once again, a moment like that reinforced how the pilgrimage should be shared as much as possible. Strangers from around the world interacting with each other and providing support, love, and friendship.

After many courses of Italian food, as well as a fresh addition to my menu of likes, octopus. A last embrace occurred; I departed my new friends. Only a few moments passed outside when I came across my friends from North Carolina. They informed me bedbugs afflicted them last night, a nightmare of mine. I pleasantly maintained a distance as we spoke. I mentioned I would pray for their safety and quick recovery.

With evening upon the city, mass began shortly. I attended the beginning per usual, exited during Communion. As always, I could not understand the language spoken. However, as I let the words wash over me, I allowed myself to listen to my heart. I believed it knew all things. Under the spiritual shelter, I told myself to cherish and savor each moment.

Four days until Santiago, wow!!

Portomarin to Palas de Rei

CHAPTER 37

OCTOBER 7TH, 2012

The goal of today was Palas de Rei, about 25 kilometers (15-plus miles). I planned on taking a detour to view the Vilar de Donas.

I started earlier than expected that morning. The night sky remaining visible upon departure. I tried to force myself into later starting times to ensure I enjoyed the landscapes and treasures along the way. As normal, I found myself in solitude and walked in silence.

I chose the two-and-a-half-kilometers detour to the church, San Salvador in Vilar de Donas, considered a national monument and an ancient seat of the Knights of Santiago. Built in the 14th century, the church offered excellent relics and possessed stone effigies of the Vilar de Donas knights.

I observed each relic in detail. The quiet atmosphere was divine. As I viewed the carvings, my mind drifted to a passage I have read from Paulo Coelho:

"I sensed I was living two lives at once. In one, I was obliged to do all the things I had to do as well as fight for ideas in which I did not believe. I had to pay the bills. My other life was my dream life, lessons I have learned through reading along with encounters with people who share the desire to live a free life. I want those two lives to draw near. I believe and trust my dreams eventually shall take over my everyday life."

The afternoon approached as I reached Palas de Rei. For being Sunday, almost everything was closed. Though, as I arrived in the town, I had a laugh. On the road outside of a bar, someone had parked a John Deere 2030 tractor. I guess the person either lost the keys to the car or I have returned to rural Mississippi. It made this Country Boy smile. My uncle worked for John Deere, and another uncle used the same tractor on his Mississippi farm. I located the albergue of my choice. It was the first albergue I stayed in with no closing hours, but they required travelers to depart by 8:00 A.M. the next morning. *Too bad was not in a city like Leon,* I thought, *I could have stayed out all night if I chose.* Approaching the bed area, the newer pilgrims were in their bunks resting from their grueling, first days on the Camino.

As day transitioned into night, I curled into my sleeping bag. I used the time for rest, contemplation, and some meditation. I loved the simple life I was currently involved with.

I recalled a passage I read before departing on my adventure. It centered on how people are afraid to pursue their most important dreams, because they feel they do not deserve them, or they cannot achieve them. I trusted the fear of suffering was worse than the suffering of trying itself. I believed regret was worse than failure. I reinforced I was doing the right thing assuming by performing the pilgrimage, I allowed myself to encounter God. I have discovered things along the way which I never would have seen had I not had the courage to risk it all. My eyes have seen the landscapes of France and Spain, my hands have touched stone walls built in the early centuries, and my feet have trekked where millions have gone before me. For a country boy from Zama, Mississippi, population 36, it seemed impossible to achieve. Yet, here I am on the Camino de Santiago, on the quest for St. James. Anything was possible. Just dream it, and, most importantly, act on it. I drifted off to deep sleep. My dreams carrying me forward.

Palas de Rei to Ribadiso

CHAPTER 38

OCTOBER 8TH, 2012

I began at dawn for Ribadiso, a 28.5-kilometer (18-mile) trek. As I departed, a light rain descended. The beads of droplets repelled from the blue rain jacket. I observed the cleansing of the surroundings. Not only was nature's garbage being transported away but the same rain acted as nourishment for the growing seeds.

I walked through a patch of eucalyptus which had a wonderful aroma. I stopped at the Igrexa Santiago in Obento, where the parish priest offered a blessing for me. I observed delicate flowers and ate a hand-picked pear today. Though the rain increased, it did not detour the peaceful sensations of my day.

Tonight, as I laid in the albergue resting, thoughts were whirling inside my mind. They rambled from music to writing and traveling. I cannot wait to play and hear my guitar as I love music. I desired to perform on stage, write a book about the pilgrimage, and allow others a glimpse into my journey. I desired to travel and see the world with my backpack and an open spirit wanting to taste, see, feel, and smell unknown experiences. I really enjoyed being in the woods surrounded by the peaceful sounds of nature.

I maintained unwavering faith the pilgrimage was the correct choice. It was what I strongly believed God wanted for me. I desired to listen to my inner voice, my soul, and to God. I continued to pray, have faith, and hope looking forward to the next chapter in my life. I wanted the pilgrimage to be the transition into my next phase, feel each day anew, like a journey and adventure. I wanted to feel inspired and inspire others acting as a light.

Ribadiso to Arca O Pina

CHAPTER 39

OCTOBER 9TH, 2012

I awoke to the sounds of a steady rain as I listened to the drops tap upon the roof. The destination today was Arca O Pino, about 22 kilometers (13-plus miles) away.

Outside of the Casa Calzada, a man sold fresh strawberries he had grown. I craved some, however, I did not want to spend any euros. When he asked if I wanted a portion of strawberries, I declined by saying I had no money. He grinned and held out a green basket filled with ripened, red strawberries. He allowed me to have some for free. When I only picked out five strawberries, he chuckled and gave me two handfuls. The precious gift from the stranger renewed my body and spirit. The strawberries were sweet and delicious. With each bite, I savored the taste and thankful for his generosity.

After a wet, muddy day, I arrived in Arca O Pina at the end of the afternoon. It was the last major town before Santiago. I checked into the albergue and relaxed after my shower, to warm my bones from the wet chill.

Darkness appeared over the land. I retreated to my bunk and listened to music. The melodies on the instrumentals vibrated through my ear canals, producing chills along my skin. The tiny hairs of my arms were standing upward. It produced an instant thought, *I wanted to perform songs, hear people clap along, sing to my lyrics, and applaud afterwards. Was music or writing in my future?* I have a creative soul. Perhaps, I missed my true calling. Was it too late in life to chase childhood dreams?

Staring up at the tiled ceiling, a lightning bolt of thoughts sparked through my mind. I was an introvert. I was a vast melting pot of possibilities. I was a seeker. I wanted to feel life and create a dream life. Through self-reflection, pursuit, quest of knowledge, and a journey of wisdom my soul would become golden. I may shed tears, encounter love and loss, but I would continue to live life with desire and passion. Truth, inspiration, and creativity were the goals. The sounds of nature, the silence of the Universe, and the whisper of my inner voice shall be my teachers. Pain, loss, and failure shall materialize. But hope and faith would continue me along the path I choose.

Arca O Pina to Santiago

CHAPTER 40

OCTOBER 10TH, 2012

I awoke overflowing with excitement and gratitude. Santiago, home to St. James, sat only 20 kilometers (12-plus miles) away. I decided to not leave before dawn with the many pilgrims who would try to make noon mass at the Cathedral. Instead, I cherished the walk and would attend the Pilgrim's Mass tomorrow.

As I stepped away from the albergue, the skies produced a misty rain. I chose not to wear my rain gear, instead I reveled in the refreshing cleansing from Mother Nature. The pathway through the peaceful woods were slick at times while the aroma of eucalyptus filled the air.

Throughout today, there were plenty of monuments, statutes, and churches to gaze upon. As I entered the city limits, elation overwhelmed me. Though it changed to, *where in the world was the Cathedral?* I perceived myself on a mission, like a secret agent. Tunnel vision ensued to reach my ultimate destination. After about three kilometers into the city of Santiago, I reached the Praza Obradoiro and the

Cathedral. Leading up to that moment I thought as I saw the Cathedral, my eyes would fill with tears. However, my first thought was: *I would see you later or tomorrow, let me go get my Compostela.*

I arrived at the Pilgrim's Office noticing a line of about 150 pilgrims ahead of me. I recognized a few of them. As I stood in line, waiting my turn, I thought about the thousands of pilgrims who had completed the journey. The line moved swiftly, and soon I stood before the person who would grant me my Compostela. She looked over my stamps, verified I walked at least 100 kilometers and asked why I chose the Camino. After my explanation of wanting to hear God's voice, I received the final stamp and my Compostela.

I went across the street to the private hotel. As I entered my room, I fixated on the queen bed and bathroom which were all mine. The window allowed observation of the principal street below. I unpacked everything from my backpack and relished in a long hot shower. Over 500 miles washed away with those beads of water.

Sitting in a tranquil state, a rainstorm brewed outside. The droplets began pounding off the windowpane, creating tranquil melodies. As I listened to the rain fall, surprisingly, still not a lot of emotions churned. Perhaps, I needed some time to relax and allow the moment to saturate my soul. I thought I would cry my eyes out by now because of the emotional overload. Instead, I remained quiet, alone, and comfortable.

Santiago

CHAPTER 41

OCTOBER 11TH, 2012

I tossed and turned throughout last night. I arose groggy, as the early sunrise woke me prematurely. Rubbing my eyes and arching my back, I prepared for the big day.

I entered the Cathedral through the "Gate of Glory" around 7:30 A.M. The sculpture by the entrance represented the history of Salvation with passages from the Old and New Testament carved into the darkened, ancient stone. In a smaller section of the Cathedral, morning mass took place. The atmosphere soothing and intimate. I roamed around for a handful of minutes, gazing upon the different statues and murals. Instead of finishing my self-guided tour, I was drawn to a pew and watched the rest of morning mass. My eyes experienced no immediate tears or raging joy, but I had one sensation: peace.

After morning mass completed, it was time to be introduced to St. James. His tomb was located down a few steps in a private room under the main alter. The room itself allowed two people to kneel on slightly raised stools covered in red fabric. Behind those, enough room for three, maybe four people to lean against the back wall to view the tomb. His remains were inside a silver urn, the size of a small casket. The urn sat on a concrete foundation a few feet high with carvings on the front of the concrete base appearing to be two doves drinking from the same cup. The Apostle Saint James was an intimate friend of Jesus Christ. His favorite statement, "Death has been defeated, Jesus Christ has been resurrected."

In the presence of St. James, I sensed joy. The kneeling man next to me and behind me had tears in their eyes, though my eyes remained dry. During my moment with St. James, the man kneeling to my left gave me a piece of paper with Jesus on it. His generosity sparked my heart, marveling at how generosity continued upon my Camino. After a few moments of prayer and pondering, I exited.

The Pilgrim's Mass began in an hour. I located a seat an hour early, to ensure I may have the best view possible. The services began, and, at first, I thought I had picked the wrong seat. It seemed about one thousand, or more, people stood instead of sitting in the low seated chairs blocking my view of the altar, being only five foot six, I could not see the priest. Thankfully, everyone sat as the priest prepared to swing the Botafumeiro, suddenly I could see. As the Botafumeiro swung back and forth under the power of eight priests, incense filled the air, tears flowed freely from my eyes.

Upon the termination of the Pilgrim's Mass, I saw Michael from Germany. We had lunch. We discussed our agendas. It turned out both of us were heading onto Finis-terre and Muxia tomorrow. We decided to go together. We set up our departure time and went our separate ways.

As dusk returned, I revisited the Cathedral, though it had a clashing atmosphere the second time. Filled with tourist groups, each group had a tour guide holding a microphone with a dozen followers. The entire ambience had changed from the peace I experienced earlier in the day to annoyance. There were flash bulbs, talking, and bags shuffling in all directions. To escape, I stepped upstairs to visit the St. James statue. I placed my head upon his shoulders and thanked him, along with Jesus, for helping me complete my pilgrimage.

Santiago to Negreira

CHAPTER 42

OCTOBER 12TH, 2012

I departed that morning for the ocean with my friend Michael. We exited at dawn. Before we withdrew Santiago, Michael and I looked upon the Cathedral and said one last prayer. *Thank you, Lord, for granting me the strength, persistence, and patience to complete the Camino de Santiago. I ask for continued guidance as I proceed on the way. I ask for protection for Michael and myself as we complete the loop back to Santiago.*

Michael and I followed the clam shells and yellow arrows toward a new destination.

It took a few kilometers to reacquaint myself to wearing the backpack again. There was only a handful of pilgrims leaving that morning for the ocean journey. The route from Santiago to Finisterre was 260 kilometers and then another 29 kilometers to Muxia. The distance from Santiago to Muxia was about the same as to Finisterre. It would take about three-to-four days to reach Finisterre, then one day to Muxia.

We walked almost the entire route together today. Largely, filled with a comfortable silence. Most of the day was on natural paths with a few high climbs. We crossed a medieval bridge in Augapesada. Looking across the water, I could see sections of waterfalls in the distance, reminding me of a smaller Niagara Falls. Later on, we came across a patch of eucalyptus trees. Michael handed me some leaves he crumbled up in his hand. I inhaled the aroma. It was like inhaling a cough drop.

In Carballo, a generous Spanish woman provided us with freshly picked grapes. She grew them in her backyard. The skins of the grapes were bitter, but the juice refreshing. *I bet she would use those grapes for some homemade wine in the future.*

Michael and I talked during a restful break. We decided to follow the path to Finisterre first then end in Muxia. We would return by bus to Santiago. I liked the idea, because in the movie *The Way* the father's journey ended in Muxia. Mr. Sheen's character spread his son's ashes into the ocean there. The ritual allowed him to have final closure of his son's death. It was fitting. The movie was the initial inspiration for my decision, and I would have closure to my pilgrimage in the same location.

As I laid in my bunk bed that evening, I reflected about the people in my life asking, "Why are you doing this?" I brushed away the thought. I understood I did not have to give them a reason why. No matter what they thought. It did not matter. I am responsible for my life. It was up to me to live my best life. I am free to choose my destiny.

I thought about the handful of people I met along the way. When I asked if they would repeat the Camino over again, they said, "not in a million years." It actually took me back. I totally desired to repeat it in my lifetime. I have enjoyed my pilgrimage. Of course, I have had pain and the unknown aspects of my future were difficult to bear. However, my personal growth outweighed the rest. I imagined the new unwavering courage stirring in me. It was the adventure of a lifetime. I had strengthened a pure sense of existence and observed life from a fresh perspective. I forged a new energy in the name of a clearer future; one on my terms.

Negreira to Beyond Olveiroa

CHAPTER 43

OCTOBER 13TH, 2012

I remained in bed, laughing to myself, as everyone surrounding me rustled to depart early as I was the last pilgrim to exit around 8:00 A.M. I regretted leaving all of those days at 5:00 A.M. My mind drifted to all the scenery I may have missed gazing upon.

A chilly morning covered in a curtain of fog was present when I stepped out from the albergue. My vision impaired past two football fields. I adjusted my backpack straps, preparing for the 35-kilometer jaunt. Most of the morning had an eerie, horror-movie atmosphere with the sun rising through the dense fog. At any moment, Jason or Freddie could have slashed me from the dense forest. Most of the stone monuments I encountered resembled structures from an Edgar Allan Poe poem. Around lunch time, the fog burnt off to reveal exquisite blue skies containing no clouds.

I heard one of the best stories for trekking the Camino. A woman from Oklahoma told it to me as we walked together. Her great-grandfather trekked the Camino in 1890, beginning in Bayonne. It took him about one year. He walked with another man from Ireland, who taught him English along the way. They would stop from time to time to work for a farmer to receive food, money, or a place to stay. After they reached Santiago, he went to Ireland with his new friend and met his future wife, a local woman living down the road. He then came to America in 1901 and had his first child in 1905. The story goes that he always wore a scalloped shell lapel pin on his suit. When she was a little girl, she heard the stories. As she got older, she realized what it all meant. She wanted the lapel pin, but her great-grandfather told her she would have to complete the Camino in order to obtain it. So, here she is, walking the Camino. Her son was supposed to walk it in the next few years. We talked about her husband who has his doctorate and worked at Oklahoma State, as a professor. She provided insightful details about her husband's experiences as a professor, since I shared, I am debating on whether to take a faculty position myself.

Overall, today was lovely with its scenery. I watched horses gallop throughout the countryside, and the section after Olveiroa was above an enormous river. I admired the windmills twirling on the distant mountain tops.

Finisterre

OCTOBER 14TH, 2012

I departed energized. By the end of the day, I would arrive in Finisterre. My rare accomplishment, as not many pilgrims who make the pilgrimage to Santiago complete the Finisterre/Muxia loop by foot delighted me.

Finisterre was a rock-bound peninsula on the west coast of Galicia, Spain. The beauty of the sea with its waves crashing against the rocks and cliffs were ravishing. In Roman times, they considered it the end of the world and a famous fishing port. They built most of the homes around the peninsula, and all shared similar tile roofing.

After returning from City Hall where I obtained the Finisterre Certificate, a colorful version of the Santiago Compostela, Michael and I connected outside the albergue. We headed toward the lighthouse, a three-kilometer path to see the "end of the world." The earlier rain cleared as the sun neared its disappearance over the sea's horizon. At sunset, we prepared an area along the rocks above the sea to perform the burning ritual. Pilgrims used the burning ritual to release ties and allow transformation. It released the past, negativity, or painful memories. Fire was a powerful symbol of wisdom, knowledge, passion, and purification. Basically, a way to free oneself and allow closure.

The flames of red, yellow, and blue waved through the sea breeze. Michael and I first uncorked a bottle of red wine. We each pressed the bottle to our lips and drank its nectar, pondering what object we would set ablaze. I burned my remaining sock liner. The thin white material scorched black quickly and created ashes. I walked over 550 miles wearing the liner. I trusted in God the next door would open. Next, Michael took his turn. Then, a girl from Denmark asked to use our flame for her personal ritual as well. A domino effect occurred. A middle-aged gentleman from Switzerland joined our circle, plus two women from Colorado, and then a few others. Our small group of two instantly became almost a dozen. Lastly, a man who trekked over 2600 kilometers burnt his shoes. It was comparable to putting a car tire on the fire as large flames with black smoke billowed toward the heavens. It reminded me of the last explosions of a fireworks show. We all sat around in silence as the first stars appeared above us.

Once again, the surrounding snoring woke me up. I went into the commons area at 3:30 A.M. Lying on a sofa in silence, my friend Joe from NC smiled as I entered. Under whispered voices we reflected on our travels and even touched on religion.

Finisterre To Muxia

CHAPTER 45

OCTOBER 15TH, 2012

The morning presented itself as Michael and I departed Finisterre towards Muxia. We took one final stroll along the beach. Half buried in the tan, soft sand, I found a shell resembling the iconic Camino scallop. I trusted it was a sign, or omen, as I placed it in my pocket. The trail rose from the sand, elevating us above Finisterre. I paused for one last look over those red-tiled roofs and the distant mountains I had ascended and descended.

The highlight of my day's experience was crossing the steppingstones of the floating rocks. They arranged those stones across a stream of mild, flowing water. Recently, a bridge was constructed over the stream. However, I wanted to follow the original Pilgrim's path. With Michael above on the bridge, I stood at the bank with bare feet. The first step into the icy water almost made me change my mind. The water's depth also much deeper than I expected. Not only did the water rise to my knees at some points but the stones were farther apart than my short strides wanted to allow. I stumbled a few times fearing a crash into the stream because the rocks were so slippery. But taking my time, one rock at a time, I finally completed the excursion. Though I was elated at my accomplishment, I understood why they built the above bridge.

The day's walk deemed difficult, but we progressed. I walked primarily alone, for my slower pace. Occasionally, I saw Michael's red sweater in the distance. My mind escaped to a higher place as the miles disappeared with little thought for the steps.

Muxia, a small, coastal town had a port where fishing boats were docked, as it reminded me of coastal towns in the Northeast of America. A storm brewed as I entered the city, causing the sea to become rough with winds strong enough to sway my body back and forth.

I bundled up in my fleece and full-body rain gear for protection. I headed to the final location from the movie *The Way*. Standing upon a concrete path, I gazed upon the turbulent seas. The water crashed into the rock sculptures formed over the centuries. The history states where I stood was the same place the Virgin Mary journeyed to encourage St. James in his preaching and evangelism. The church behind me dated back to the 12th century. With gusting winds of up to at least thirty miles per hour, the storm intensified, my rain jacket resembled a sail. The power of the sea created a feeling of being tiny, or a minor part of a bigger picture.

I wanted to throw my trekking poles into the ocean in the same way the character in the movie spreads his son's ashes. Instead, I found some solitude and threw my last

Mississippi red rock into the water and said a prayer of gratitude. The pleasure of unconstrained power leapt from my soul. Afterwards, I made a monument. I placed the golden sticks into two rocks in an X formation. Observing the creation, I finally felt my body say, *Enough, you are done.*

That night I celebrated with Michael over a pint of ale. We gave cheers to our journey and to our friendship.

CHAPTER 46

OCTOBER 16TH, 2012

The daylight unfolded much too prematurely. I arose reluctantly, feeling lethargic. That morning, I would step onto a bus and return to Santiago. It has been almost forty days since my transportation was anything else but my own two feet. I gathered my belongings and exited the albergue to wait for the bus. As the silver-and-blue tin can approached, spewing odors of diesel fuel, I held my breath. I climbed the three metal steps. Once seated, the driver hit the accelerator, and we were off. It was weird. I felt like I sat in a foreign object because it was moving so hurriedly. As it retraced my steps, town to town, in a blur, I knew it would have taken me hours to walk the same route.

As the day progressed, my mind drifted to one primary thought, *I am ready to return home.* The trip had been worth every step. If I had the time and the money, I would do those types of trips and pilgrimages full time, all over the world, and then write about it. I desired to share with others what I have found along the way. The experience had given me great blessings, amazing generosity, and life lessons.

One lesson, I needed to clean up my life and remove the unneeded clutter. Everything I needed could comfortably rest upon my shoulders. The Camino-style living over the past few weeks made me fully appreciate what I had and what I needed.

My desire to travel reinforced. There was beauty everywhere, especially with no agenda and by foot. It was so stimulating to see what was around the next bend, or over the next hill, or to see who I might interact with in the next town. I wanted to see and taste the world.

That evening, I remained still in my bed. I realized the Camino helped me let go of the constructs of days and hours. It allowed me to focus more on the present moment, which was the most important moment.

CHAPTER 47

COMING HOME

As I said goodbye to St. James, I trusted, no matter how far from Santiago I may be, it was forever imprinted on my soul. I perceived I could do whatever I focused my mind to. Simply, do it was the new rule. By accomplishing my pilgrimage, I learned I could push myself onto fantastic feats in all facets of my life. There were no challenges too big for me to take on. I set out to accomplish something bold, and I had done exactly that.

"Carry in your memory, for the rest of your life, the splendid things that came out of those difficulties. They will serve as a proof of your abilities and will give you confidence when you are faced by other obstacles." — Unknown

I exited the airport on Florida soil. My oldest brother opened the door for my backpack. I slid into the front seat. His first question, "What's next?" I snapped my seatbelt into place and explained my fresh vision. With each fresh day, I wished to sense more through my emotions. I desired to increase my creative energy and to explore options. I craved to be an inspiration to the world. I yearned to write, tell stories, compose music, draw, color, and blog. With each mile closer to my home, tears flowed from my eyes.

CHAPTER 48

As I conclude this book, eight years after "A Quest of St. James," I want to include a snapshot of what happened after.

Instead of taking a risk and attempting something visionary, I shut the inner voice out again. I followed the hamster wheel hoping for a different outcome, insanity I know. I departed Florida for Mississippi about four weeks after I returned from my pilgrimage taking the faculty position. I remained a college professor for about three years. In 2016 the inner voice finally returned becoming so loud I could not take it. So, I took another leap of faith. I resigned the position in January 2016. Read "**Rambling Across America**" to discover what happened next.

It was easy for me to believe that what you desired was no less than what you deserved, to assume if you want something badly enough, it was your God-given right to have it. Perhaps I mistake passion for insight, and acted according to an obscure, gap-ridden logic. I thought my journey would fix all that was wrong with my life. However, it took me applying what I had learned from my journey and a leap of faith to fix it.

I hope you have enjoyed the journey.
May it have sparked something inside of you to find your own adventure.

For Further Information:

American Pilgrims on the Camino
1514 Channing Avenue
Palo Alto, CA 94303
www.americanpilgrims.com

ABOUT THE AUTHOR

Tommy Ray, born in 1973, from Zama Mississippi, population 36 people. He followed the red dusty dirt road to receive three degrees, each one taking him closer to ever-changing dreams.

However, no matter what he achieved, he always had a voice inside of him telling him he desired to live his life through an original voice. For many years he ignored the voice to follow other endeavors, but the voice was always there and increasing in volume.

The voice encouraged Tommy to resign a stable job to go on his pilgrimage along the Camino de Santiago in 2012. A pilgrimage in the footsteps of St. James through France and Spain. Though when he returned, he shut the voice out again and returned to the secured norm like so many of us do. In 2016, the voice finally became so loud, he could not take it, he took another leap of faith. He resigned another position in January 2016 and journeyed on a self-guided music tour, the "Confessions of a Dreamer Tour." Read "**Rambling Across America**" for the details.

He writes and became an author to create value and inspiration to the world desiring all to leave their mark, thinks big, as well as never give up on their dreams. He has always been inspired by travel adventure tales of real-life journeys. He decided it was how he desired to spend his life.

His "Country Boy" travel adventure books, are written in a journal style, providing insights and glimpses of his fear, pain, joy, and the love which his travels have brought. The goal, to assist readers in dreaming big, listening to their hearts along with trusting their instincts. To take a leap of faith.

I invite you to continue keeping up with me at:
www.tommyraybooks.com

Do Not Miss Future Adventures with Tommy Ray

I ask and invite you to leave a review on the purchasing
website as well as Goodreads.

"Country Boy Travel Series"

Short stories to allow a glimpse into the nightmares of
Tommy Ray

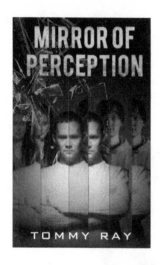

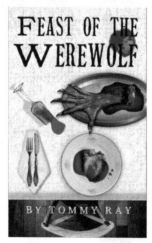

"The man who follows the crowd will usually go no further than the crowd. The man who walks alone is likely to find herself in places no one has ever been before."
—*Francis Phillip Wernig*

CPSIA information can be obtained
at www.ICGtesting.com
Printed in the USA
LVHW041704131120
671369LV00004B/294